iPhone 12
CAMERA USER GUIDE

A Complete Step By Step Tutorial And Guide On How To Use The iPhone 12, Pro And Pro Max Camera For Beginners And Professional Cinematic Videography With Tips And Tricks

By

George wind

Table Of Contents

CHAPTER ONE

INTRODUCTION

From the outside, you would not believe that the camera part of the iPhone 12 has changed a lot. The two rear lenses are similar to the previous year's model and offer wide and extremely wide optical support through 12-megapixel sensors.

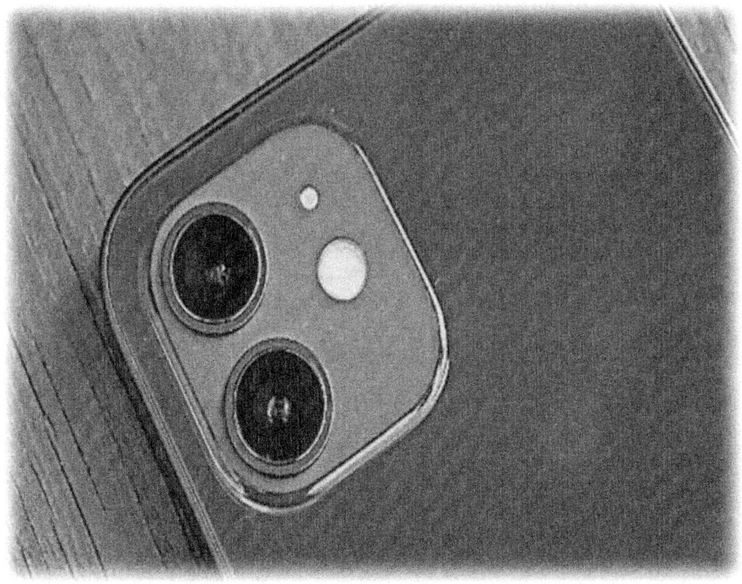

Don't let your eyes fool you when upgrades are being made. In particular, the main camera now has a new 7-element design with the largest aperture / 1.6 on the iPhone. The result of both changes is a 27% improvement in low-light performance. This leads to details and the further development of Smart HDR and Deep Fusion under the most adverse conditions.

So let's start with some night mode shots that show how the iPhone behaves in low light over the course of a year. Both photos create dramatic, impressive night scenes, but the iPhone 12's performance is a bit more intense. This shows how the stone absorbs the light from the above lamps, with more realistic shadows covered with shadows on the stone and better sensitivity in the tones of the mirror. The newer iPhone 11 Pro doesn't lose much, however.

However, Apple needs some work. Given the best performance of the iPhone 12 compared to Pixel 5 in the example above, it seems that Google has an overnight advantage. Although Apple software pushes the boundaries of objects and gives everything a deeper frame, Google algorithms usually give a more visible result with much less overall noise. It is not visible in the pixel image at the edges of the iPhone 12.

In daylight, the main camera of the iPhone 12 gives you a little charm. While the Note 20 captured this idyllic lake landscape a little more intensely, especially with remote trees, I prefer the iPhone 12 with the most realistic color rendering, from the dark blue afternoon sky to the surrounding yellow, orange, and green water. Samsung is exaggerating here with post-processing, as is tradition.

However, if we lift the well to the right, the iPhone 12's limitations seem painful. The iPhone 12 doesn't have optical zoom - you'll have to spend more on the iPhone 12 Pro or Pro Max. But even then we couldn't see the Note 20 crystal balls, the waves on the surface of the lake and the striking 3x hybrid zoom that holds a wall in the background.

Here we now see the lake we saw from the extremely large lenses on the iPhone 12 and OnePlus 8T for $ 749. Both shots are lost in different ways. The iPhone 12 breaks the white balance and creates a green invasion of water and clouds, while the OnePlus 8T photo is not sharp enough and spoils the surrounding image.

This fall-themed photo is complemented by two portraits of my colleague Jesse taken on the iPhone 12 and Pixel 5. Interestingly, the iPhone 12 has a wider perspective by default than the Pixel 5, which uses auto-cropping.

Still, the iPhone 12 version looks a bit more intense and handles Jesse's skin tone better. Smart HDR gently adjusts the contrast between the deep shadows covering her right shoulder and the rest of the hood.

To test the capabilities of Apple's Deep Fusion feature, which supports detailed scenes in twilight scenarios, I took a snapshot of an image using the iPhone 12 and Pixel 5. Deep Fusion is designed to combine different lights of different lengths for optimal sharpness. However, I was surprised that Google Phone creates the most expensive edition here, designing a screen texture with a resolution that the iPhone 12 cannot handle. However, when it comes to color rendering in general, I think the iPhone ultimately delivers a more attractive picture, which adds to the warmth it creates on a red, white, and neutral background.

A better example of Deep Fusion at work could be this selfie I took when the sun was going down. Here in my sweater, the iPhone 12 showed individual fibers in terms of fullness and hue compared to the blurry front camera output. The iPhone 12 12MP surprisingly captures more detail than the Note 20's 10MP sensor, but even Apple algorithms don't confuse shadows and since Samsung doesn't balance the contrast on my face. If I had to post one of these on Instagram it wouldn't be difficult to choose.

Overall, the iPhone 12 ranks first for the price range in terms of camera performance, but it isn't the best in all scenarios. However, I prefer a pixel that can capture the same demanding scenes with less noise for night photography.

CHARACTERISTICS

Apple first introduced the Smart HDR 3 update with these new phones. Part of it is a new method of recognizing scenes that will help some photos depending on the picture content. For example, it can illuminate a portrait, adjust color and contrast in a food photo, or increase the saturation in a horizontal shot.

HDR is still available independently, but you can turn off scene detection in the camera settings if you wish.

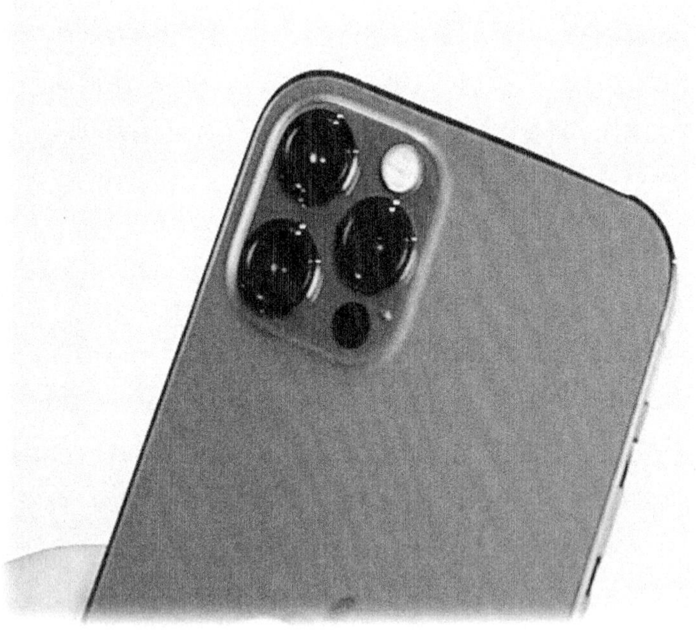

Then Deep Fusion Apple had a magical computer photo and so far only worked with large lenses. It now works with extremely wide cameras and selfies. Without user interaction, all downloads made with them will automatically look better.

Apple ProRAW is a new form of image processing that the iPhone 12 Pro and iPhone 12 Pro Max will introduce with software updates in the coming months. It combines the advantages of RAW photography like extra details in light and shadow with the advantages of Apple photography features like Smart HDR 3 and Deep Fusion.

With previous phones and iPhones, users had to choose between Deep Fusion and HDR or RAW capture. Users no longer need to do this. Deep Fusion and HDR are used, but these additional editing details are retained.

Regardless of what photo you take, Apple places great emphasis on the camera app and always tries to get the best possible frame.

♥ Portraits and aperture

It's great for portraits, and in general, iPhone cameras are made for that. These are adorable pictures for people so I think that unlike other smartphone brands, portrait photography still has its power. Just because you have a telephoto lens you usually have better portraits because the telephoto lens is less distorted when you take portraits. This is a combination of selecting and editing this camera lens.

♥ Focal Lengths

Wide: 12 MP, aperture 1.6, dual OIS

Extremely wide: 12 MP, aperture 2.4, 120 degree field of view

Tele: 12 MP, aperture 2.2, dual OIS

Optical zoom: 2.5 times zoom, 2 times zoom, 5 times optical zoom

Digital zoom: Up to 12x digital zoom

Night mode: wide, extremely wide

Features and Functions: Portrait Mode, Night Mode, LiDAR Scanner, Smart HDR 3, Deep Fusion Processing, Panorama, Dolby Vision, Apple ProRAW ("Coming Soon")

♥ Light, colors, and details

You will notice the details in these images in the light because the camera deals with well-lit scenes. The colors look right.

The iPhone also depends on the sedentary lifestyle. It is the same object of photography with three different focal lengths. Even by customizing these various elements with different textures, transparencies, and colors, the iPhone 12 Pro Max camera was durable. Fluorescent pink keeps its color and details on wooden objects are clearly defined.

♥ Flash mode and night mode

The night flash was perfect in portrait format. The flash wasn't very intense and the combination with portrait mode was flattering.

The low light auto focus is very fast [via the new LiDAR sensor] but I don't think that's a feature I was missing. Bad interior lighting has proven to be good.

♥ Edit

As with the iPhone, editing is very easy for the user. I saw that a lot of details were lost when I took the picture a little longer. However, I did enjoy editing the screen. The screen size [6.7 inches] is here.

♥ Video

The recording rate with HDR video / Dolby Vision is available. The iPhone's optical image stabilization handled many settings perfectly, with almost no flicker. The color and detail were always great and when the HDR video was turned off the difference was huge, with much less detail in visible and low light.

IPHONE 12 CAMERA POSSIBILITIES

The camera app for iPhone 12 and iPhone 12 Pro has been updated to take advantage of the latest Apple features such as night portrait and Dolby Vision HDR recording. See how you can get the most out of the camera.

The camera app on the iPhone 12 has a lot of features that Apple hasn't told most of you. Apple is focused on finding the most commonly used features to simplify and maintain the camera.

Aside from these, there are more ways and means to use them. Each one is supposed to make photography more practical, more powerful and much faster.

♥ Volume buttons

For example, this speed tip is often used by many, and some may not be familiar with this practical trick yet. With Apple, users can use the volume buttons as natural triggers in the camera app. Every time you open the camera app, you activate the shutter and take a photo every time you press any key.

If you hold down any key, the video recording will start. The video will be recorded as long as you hold down the button.

Turn down the volume but start recording video immediately

If you don't want it at all, you can change it. Go to Settings and adjust the volume key to take a photo. Choose this option. If you press and hold the volume up button, it will take photos one at a time until you release them.

♥ Other Quicktake options

This option to press the volume up button to record video is a change from what Apple calls QuickTake. Overall, QuickTake is a quick way to take a single photo, video, or batch.

In the camera app, press the white shutter button once to take a photo. Touch and hold the button and you will now start recording video without stopping what you are doing and switch to video mode.

When you do this, the middle button will change from white to red. Stops video recording as soon as you release the shutter button.

This is great for very fast videos, but not practical when recording longer scenes. If you don't want to continue recording video and always want to press the shutter button, you can hold down the button and then slide it to the right. It will lock in video mode and you can lift your finger off the glass.

If you immediately press and drag left, it will start the download in quick mode until you stop.

You need to get used to how these two different functions are performed. Still, they are a much faster way to get these shots without going far ahead.

♥ Aspect ratio

The aspect ratio of the recorded image can be easily changed. When you press the carrot icon at the top of the camera app, the tool tray will appear above the trigger. Find the aspect ratio that matches what you are dragging and make other decisions.

With Apple, you can take pictures in 4: 3, 16: 9, and 1: 1 frame.

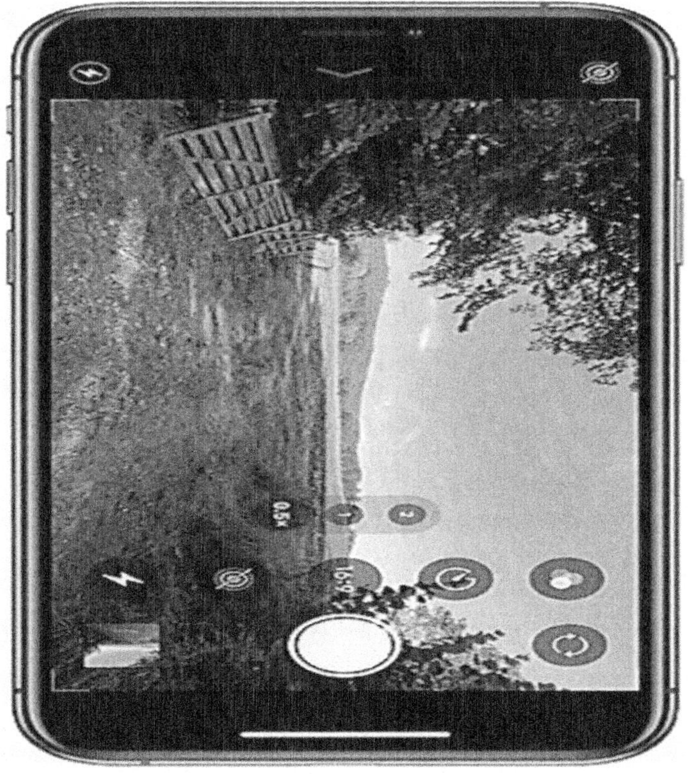

If you take a 16: 9 photo and later decide that you don't want a widescreen, you can crop it to 4: 3 in the Photos app. But without any loss of quality, this happens.

♥ Reach Adjustment

The iPhone 12 and iPhone 12 mini have two cameras, ultra-wide-angle and wide-angle lenses. In the camera application, you can achieve up to 0.5x with an extremely wide-angle lens or digitally zoom from 1x to 5x.

Press the 1X icon to quickly switch from 1X to .5X and back. You can also hold your finger and slide left and right to open the wheel at a closer magnification.

The iPhone 12 series is different. This is because instead of three cameras, they offer extremely large, large, and calf lenses.

Instead of a zoom display, the camera app shows the options .5X, 1X and 2X and selects an iPhone switch between the three cameras. You can also switch between the digital zoom from 0.5 to 10x.

When you're done setting the range, drag the wheel down to hide it and return to the quick switches.

♥ Portrait mode

Portrait mode has been around for a while and Apple continued to improve it. Over the years we could customize different zoom levels, front camera options, different lighting effects and bezels in reality.

You can now activate portrait mode with different levels of bokeh in the background.

Close the lens to put the phone in portrait mode at night

The lens cover makes the phone allow portraits in night mode

There is a significant new feature for the iPhone 12 Pro and iPhone 12 Pro Max. Vertical images can now be taken in low light thanks to the LiDAR scanner. With LiDAR, the camera can quickly focus on almost any light.

Portraits in night mode can only be taken at 1X. If you try to take photos in low light with 2X, the icon in the lower left corner will prompt you to switch to 1X. When night mode is activated, a night mode icon will appear in the top left corner.

♥ Night operation

Speaking of night mode, it's now enabled on all lenses. Night mode can be used for self-portraits and very large, wide and telephoto cameras.

Night mode will turn on automatically when the light comes on. However, you can also turn it on and off manually. When we get close to the above ratio, you'll see it on the toolbar. Usually, the appropriate shutter speed is selected, but you can set the slider faster or slower. These numbers vary depending on how far the phone has moved.

When you place the phone on a tripod, night mode works with shutter speeds of up to 30 seconds for great shots in low light.

New this year for the iPhone 12 and iPhone 12 Pro is the ability to save the lock in night mode. And they are activated automatically when they open a little and you start recording the time range.

♥ Dolby Vision

For video games, the ability to record in Dolby Vision HDR is a big deal. The earliest mobile phone that can edit, record, and share Dolby Vision content.

While this is a great premium feature, it is very easy to use. Just open it from the settings.

To enable Dolby Vision recording:

> ➢ Open the Settings app
> ➢ Go to the camera
> ➢ Then go to Record Video
> ➢ Turn on HDR video

Now when you record a video, Dolby Vision will be saved as HDR. You can record Dolby Vision 4K at 60 frames per second on the iPhone 12 Pro, but the iPhone is limited to 30 frames per second.

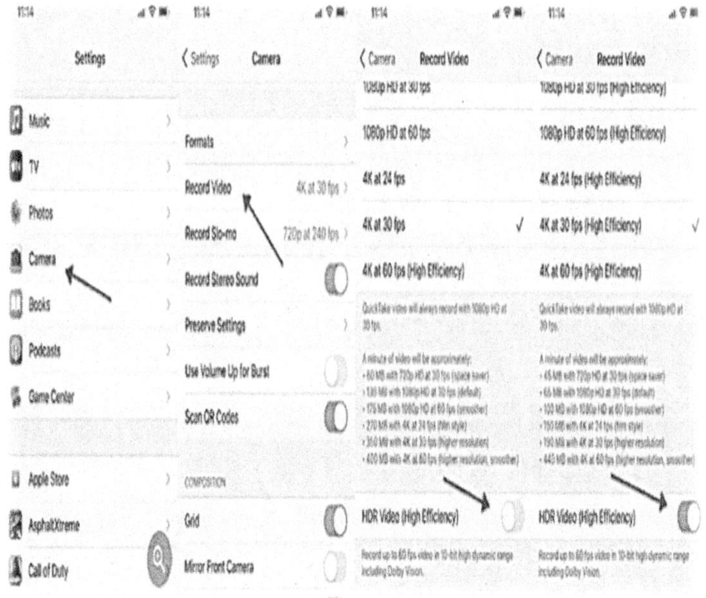

If you are recording Dolby Vision HDR video, you will see the HDR indicator in the upper left corner of the thumbnail in the photos application. HDR videos also start at normal brightness but quickly get very bright when viewed in the Photos app.

To ensure compatibility, HDR content is automatically notified based on the location and notification.

USING THE IPHONE 12 CAMERA APPLICATION

Quickly open the iPhone camera app: If your iPhone is locked, tap the screen (or the Home button on older iPhones) to turn your phone on. Then drag it to the left.

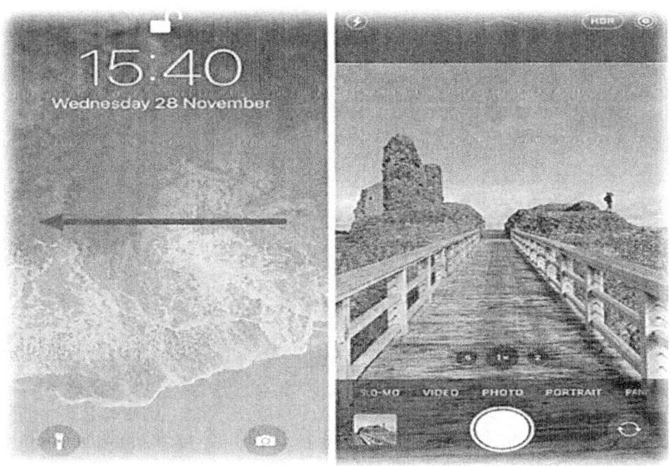

The camera app moves around the screen and you can start recording right away.

If you're already using iPhone to take pictures, turn on the camera using one of the following techniques.

> If the start screen is visible, tap the camera app icon.

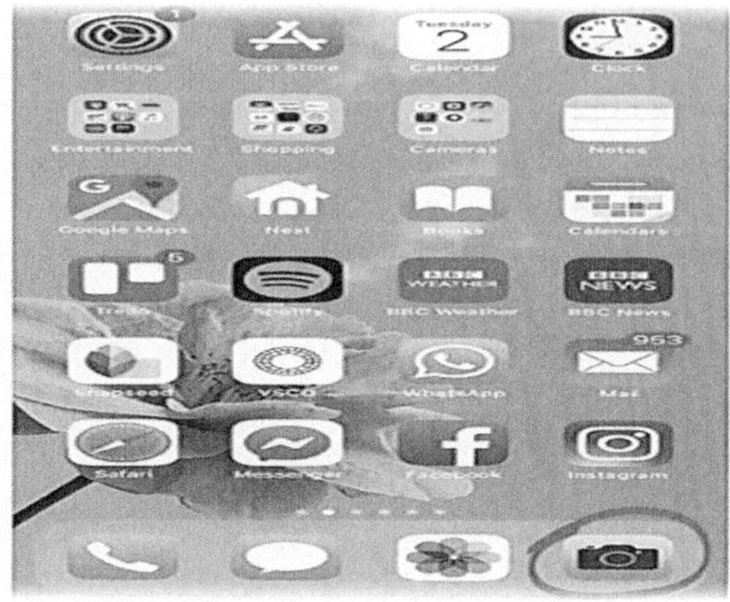

- ➤ It's a good idea to add a camera icon to the docking station at the bottom of the screen. This will make it easier to find so you can open it faster.
- ➤ Touch and hold the icon until it flashes to add a camera icon to the docking station. Drag the foot icon at the bottom of the screen. At the top right, then tap Finish.
- ➤ In the dock, be reminded that you have just four icons. If the station is already full, you must therefore first drag one of the other symbols out of the slot.
- ➤ What if you are using another application and want to open the camera quickly? You

don't need to close the application you are using.

> Instead, swipe down from the top-right corner of the screen (down from the bottom on older iPhones). This will open the Control Center, where you can tap the camera icon.

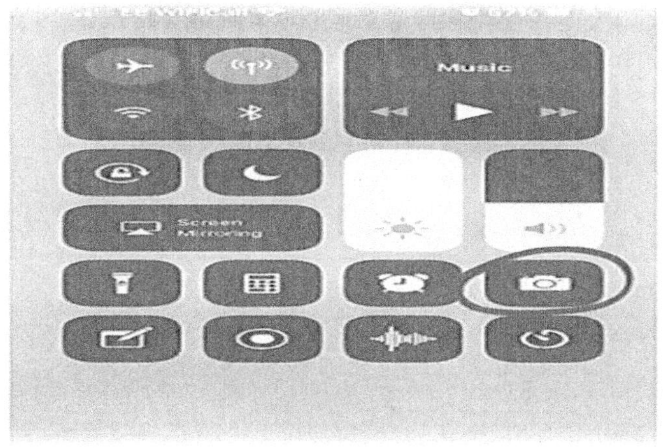

If you want to take great photos with your iPhone, you need to be prepared for a quick photo shut.

With these iPhone camera tricks, you can start recording in a second or two.

Open the camera grille for a better fit: With the iPhone camera, you can see network lines on the screen. As shown below, the grid has two horizontal lines and two vertical lines.

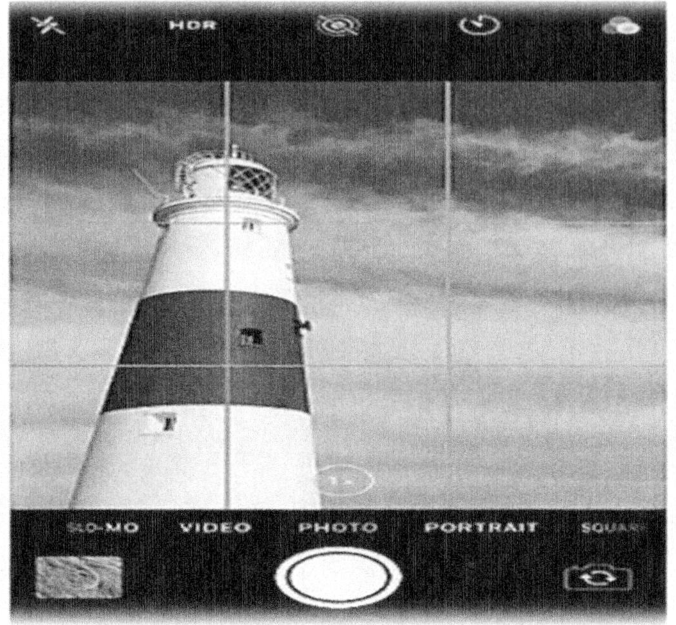

You can use these grids to create photos with better composition. This allows you to assemble the frame according to the third party rule, for example.

This rule says that it is better to place the subject off-center than in the center. Place the grid and pattern where the two fabrics meet.

When photographing the landscape, place the horizon along the top or bottom grid instead of the center.

The web is also a great tool for keeping the iPhone on par when taking photos. You can align the horizon with a horizontal grid line to keep the photo straight.

➤ To open the grid, open the Settings application and select Camera. Make sure the network is turned on (green).

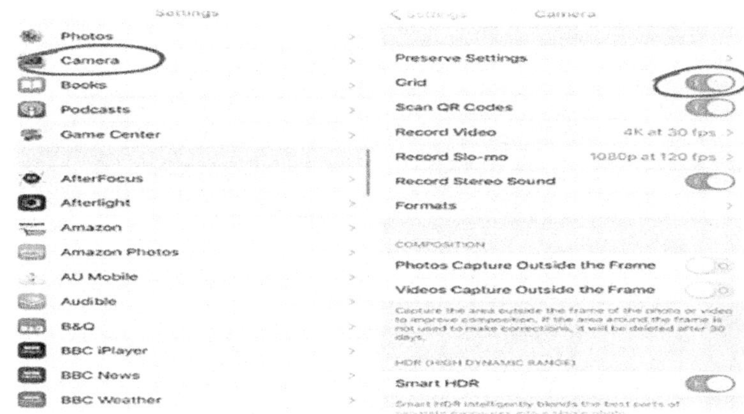

➤ Close Settings and reopen the camera application. The networks are displayed in the viewfinder.

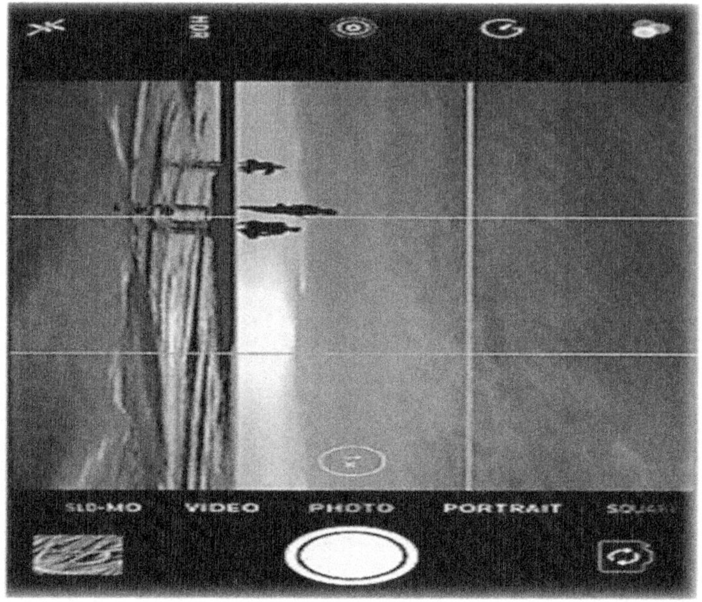

> Activating the network function also activates the synchronization tool. This tool allows you to take photos straight while shooting straight up or down.
> Ideal for food and still life photography where you have to shoot from above. Ideal if you want to take photos directly, for example, to photograph a decorative ceiling.
> If you turn the iPhone up or down, you will see a pair of white and yellow crosses in the center of the screen. When your iPhone is

parallel to the floor or ceiling, the crosses together form a yellow cross.

Choose the perfect shooting mode: IPhone's camera offers various options for taking photos and videos.

Swipe left or right at the bottom of the screen to switch between different camera modes.

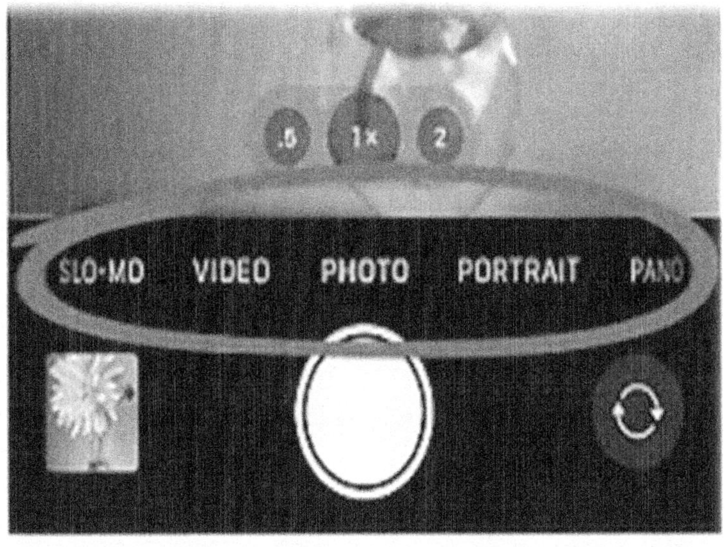

You can choose between photo, portrait, painting, video, timeout and slow motion.

There will also be a way to take square photos on the iPhone XS and older models.

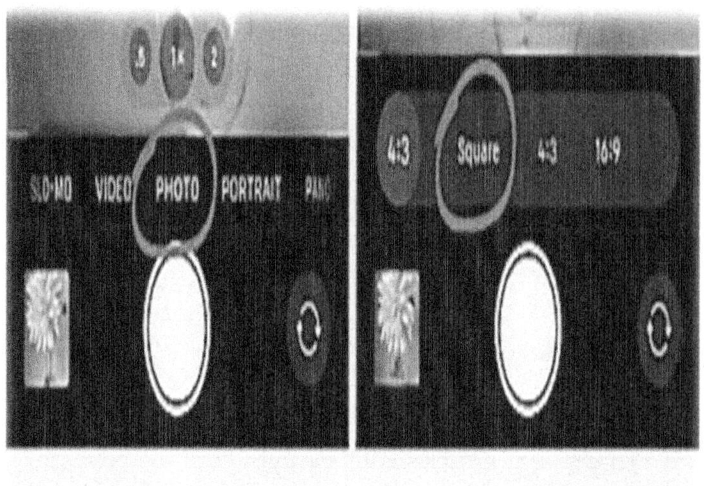

To download Square mode on iPhone 11, switch to Photo mode and tap the up arrow at the top of the screen. Touch 4: 3 at the bottom of the screen and select Square.

Purpose of various download methods

> Photo mode captures standard rectangular photos.
> The square function cuts the frame into a square shape.
> Portrait mode allows you to blur the background of your photos. Ideal for beautiful portraits of people and pets.
> Note that portrait mode is available for the new iPhone 11, iPhone 11 Pro, and iPhone

11 Pro Max. It's also available for iPhone XS, iPhone XS Max, iPhone XR, iPhone X, iPhone 8 Plus, and iPhone 7 Plus.

➢ With Pan Panorama you can take extremely panoramic shots. This is ideal for expansive landscapes and urban scenes.

➢ Hold the iPhone upright and press the shutter button to get a panorama. Move the phone around the tent in the opposite direction. Press the trigger to end the download.

➢ In video mode, you can record videos with the iPhone. Use it to make movies at home or share short videos on social media.

➢ The slow-motion mode records slow-motion videos. Ideal for slowing down fast-moving objects.

➢ Time The time-lapse video function creates time-lapse videos. Use this option to speed up the movement of slowly moving objects, such as B. Clouds moving in the sky.

How do you switch your camera between wide-angle, ultra-wide-angle and telephoto lenses:

♥ Do you have an iPhone with two or three lenses on the back?

- In this case, you can switch between zoom and zoom between iPhone camera lenses.
- The iPhone 11 Pro and iPhone 11 Pro Max have three lenses: wide-angle, ultra wide-angle, and telephoto lens.

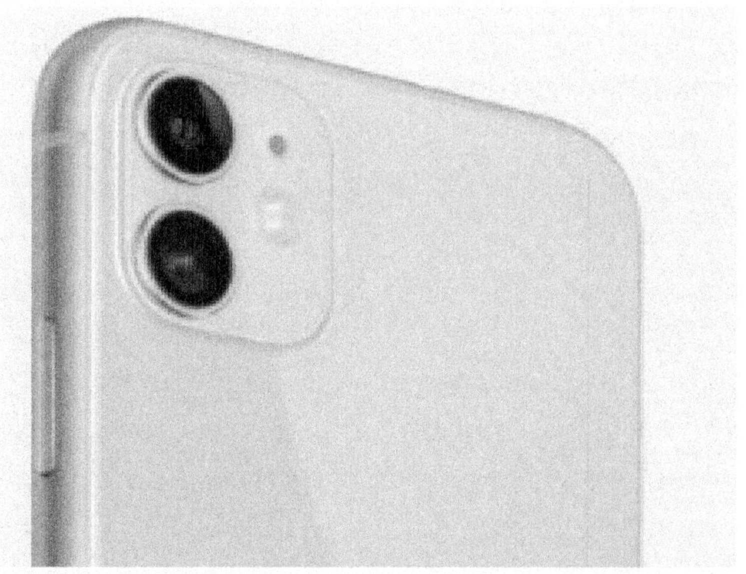

- The iPhone 11 has two lenses: wide and extremely wide.
- Older dual-lens phones have wide-angle and telephoto lenses. And the single lens iPhone has a wide angle lens.
- If you have an iPhone with two or three lenses, read below on how to switch lenses when taking photos.

- In the iPhone camera app, you will see the zoom symbols under the viewfinder.
- 0.5x is an extremely wide lens. It's a 1x wide lens. And 2x is a telephoto lens.
- Note that it only shows the numbers that match the lenses on the iPhone.
- Press 0.5 times to use the ultra wide angle lens.
- Press 1x to switch to a wide angle lens.
- Touch 2x for the telephoto lens.
- The 1x wide-angle lens has a moderately wide viewing angle. For most shooting situations, the lens is suitable.
- The extremely wide 0.5x lens has a much wider field of view. This lens allows you to shoot many scenes that are ideal for landscapes, landscapes, and tall buildings.
- The 2x telephoto lens allows you to zoom in to view distant subjects in greater detail. Perfect when you obviously can't get close to the object.

Use iPhone 11 night mode to take stunning photos in low light:

The iPhone 12 camera app has a great new feature called Night Mode!

- ♥ Night mode is a great way to capture great colors and details in photos in low light

- ♥ The great thing about night mode is that it turns on automatically when shooting in low light.

- ♥ Make sure you choose a 1x or 2x wide telephoto lens. (You cannot use night mode with the ultra-wide 0.5x lens.)

- ♥ When the light is weak enough (but not too dark), the night mode icon is white.

- ♥ This means that the night mode is not yet active ... but can be used if desired. To enable night mode, tap the white night mode icon to turn yellow.

- ♥ When the scene is bright, night mode will be activated automatically.

- ♥ The number above the yellow night mode symbol indicates the exposure time, e.g. 1 second, 3 seconds, and so on. This is the time it will take to take a photo when you press the shutter button.

- ♥ You can set the exposure time using the slider at the bottom of the screen.

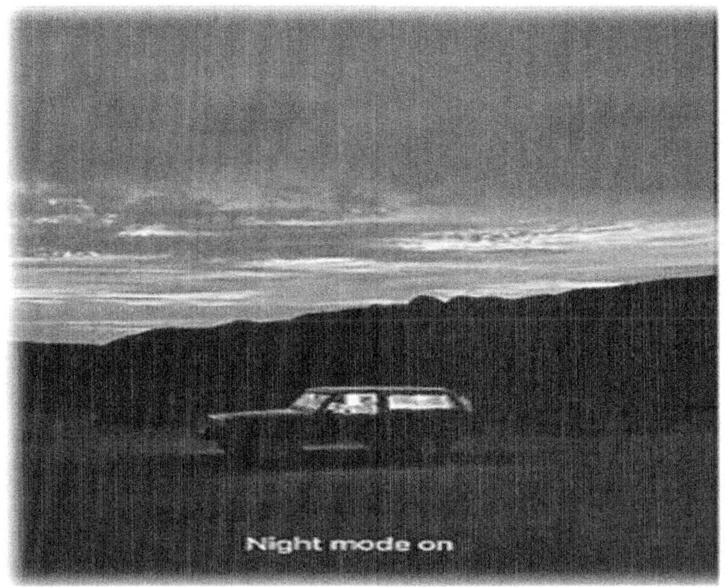

- ♥ Maximum exposure time You can use the automatic exposure time or drag the slider to the right.
- ♥ Move the slider to the left to Off to turn night mode off.
- ♥ When you're ready to take a photo, press the shutter button.
- ♥ Press and hold the iPhone until the recording is finished. The sharper your image will be when you have a more stable camera. Remember that in night mode you need some kind of light in the tent. It can be a lamp, a candle, street lights, or even car headlights.

37

- If there is no light on the stage, you will not get good results. But with a little light, you can take great night photos!
- If you are shooting in medium to low light and Night Mode is not turned on, the camera may be using Deep Fusion Mode.
- In medium and low light scenes, Deep Fusion - an automatic camera feature you can't control -, captures better textures and details.

Use the portrait function for an extremely blurred background:

Portrait mode is a great iPhone feature that will blur the background of your photos.

- Portrait mode lets you take stunning portraits of people and pets.
- Alternatively, you can use it to blur the background behind any background.
- A shallow depth of field (blurring) can usually only be achieved with a DSLR camera.
- However, in portrait mode, you can restore this effect with your iPhone.

- To take a photo in portrait mode, select Portrait from the list of graphic photo modes.
- Make sure the subject is two to eight feet from the camera. Wait for the yellow focus frame to appear around the person's face.
- When portrait mode is ready, the words Natural Light will turn yellow. (You will see the word Depth Effect on the iPhone 7 Plus.)
- You can switch between 1x wide-angle and 2x telephoto lenses on the iPhone 11 Pro and 11 Pro Max.
- When you're done, press the shutter button to take a nice portrait photo.
- Portrait mode is one of the best iPhone camera settings for taking beautiful pictures. However, in portrait mode, you can do more after taking a photo!
- You can control background blur on new iPhones (iPhone 11, 11 Pro, 11 Pro Max, XS, XS Max, and XR).
- In the photo application, open the portrait photo and press Edit.
- Click the f-number icon in the top left corner.

- The depth slider will appear under your photo. Move the slider left or right to adjust the amount of blur.
- Portrait mode also includes portrait lighting. This is a great way to add studio lighting effects to portrait photos (not available on iPhone 7 Plus).
- You can change the portrait lighting mode while shooting or after editing. Once you've taken a picture, it's easier to try different portrait lighting options.
- On the photo editing screen, tap the light portrait icon (hexagon) in the upper left corner. Portrait lighting icons appear at the bottom of your photo.
- Drag between the icons for the light portrait and select an effect, e.g. Studio light, edge light, stage light, etc.
- You can adjust the lighting effect with the slider at the bottom of the screen.
- Portrait mode is a powerful way to create professional iPhone photos. The results, however, are sometimes imperfect.
- For example, some patterns can look fuzzy when their wings need to be sharp. Or it looks sharp if the background is blurry.

- ♥ If you are not satisfied with the results, you can always remove the depth effect and return to normal view.
- ♥ Select Portrait at the top of the editing screen to do this. You can reactivate Blur at any time by pressing the portrait again.
- ♥ When you're happy with your editing, press Done to save your changes.

Use the burst function for extreme action shots:

Sequence mode is one of the hidden features of the iPhone camera that you may not even know about.

- ♥ But once you've explored the area, you'll see tremendous advances in taking pictures of moving objects.
- ♥ Burst mode takes ten photos per second while you hold down the shutter button.
- ♥ This makes it easy to get the perfect action when the object is moving across the scene.
- ♥ On the iPhone 11, 11 Pro, and 11 Pro Max, slide the shutter button to the left to activate the recording function. The camera takes a picture until you remove your finger from the screen.

- ♥ For iPhone XS and older models, just press the shutter button to take consecutive shots.
- ♥ After taking a series of pictures, you can choose the best pictures in the series and delete others.
- ♥ To choose the best pictures, open the explosion in the Photos application. Find and choose *Select* at the bottom of the screen. Select the ones you want to keep scrolling through the images.
- ♥ Click on Done. Then tap Keep only favorites.
- ♥ Use the sequence function when you're moving on stage or unpredictable.
- ♥ Ideal for photographing children, animals, birds, and water spray.
- ♥ It's also great for capturing magical moments of street photography. Try to take the perfect step or pose with the sequence function.

Take live photos to bring your pictures to life:

Live Photos are an exciting feature of the iPhone camera that will bring your photos to life.

- Live Photo creates a beautiful movie instead of instantly freezing a photo.

- It works by recording the moments before and after you took a photo. The result is a 3-second video with motion and audio.

- Here is a live photo on the beach. Click the Play button to see the movement of water and people recorded.

- Open Live Photos by tapping the Live Photos icon (circles) at the top of the Camera app. (Live photos are disabled when the icon contains a line.)

- When you press the shutter button, the camera records video 1.5 seconds before and 1.5 seconds after that time.

- If you take a live photo, play it back on the screen.

- When taking a live photo, you can use loop, reflection, or large exposure effect if necessary. To access these effects, open the live photo and drag it up.

- The loop turns your live photo into a seamless video loop. With Bounce your photo can be played live.

- Large exposure creates a stunning slow shutter effect and blurs any recorded movement. Ideal for a silky smooth effect on waterfalls and rivers.

Take photos and videos at the same time with your iPhone 12 Quicktake:

The iPhone camera app has a new feature called QuickTake.

Instead of switching to video mode to record video, you can record videos in photo mode.

To start recording the video, just hold down the shutter button. The trigger is red. A video countdown will appear at the top of the screen.

Lift your finger to stop recording the video. To continue recording video without pressing the shutter button, pull the shutter button to the right and release.

If you want, you can take a photo by pressing the white shutter button on the right while recording a video.

Press the red shutter button to stop the video recording.

Adjust the focus for sharp images:

In most cases, the iPhone autofocus is great for taking sharp pictures.

But sometimes you need more control over which part of the scene it focuses on.

Adjusting the focus is really easy

Frame the hoop and tap wherever you want with sharpness. This will usually be your main topic. A yellow square indicates the focus point.

You can lock the focus to take multiple photos with the same focus point.

To lock the focus, press and hold where you want the focus to be. When the AE / AF lock appears at the top of the screen, lift your finger.

Once the focus is locked, you can take as many photos as you want without changing the focus.

When you want to unlock the focus point, tap anywhere on your screen.

Adjusting the focus point is especially important when taking close-up pictures.

When the lens is close to the subject, you have a shallow depth of field. This means that only a small area of the scene will be in focus and the rest will be blurry.

As you can see, knowing how to take good photos with an iPhone is nice.

Adjust the lighting to the perfect brightness:

Exposure is another important feature of an iPhone camera that you should check out.

The setting relates to the brightness of a photo.

A photo that wasn't exposed looks very dark, but an overexposed photo looks too light.

A well-exposed photo has wonderful colors and details.

HOW TO CONTROL THE LIGHTING IN THE IPHONE CAMERA APPLICATION

When you press it to adjust the focus, the camera will automatically adjust the brightness of the photo. Adjusts the contact level based on the area you are touching.

If you touch the bright part of the scene, the bright parts will be correctly lit with lots of color and detail. This is a great way to avoid overexposing the sky of a landscape scene by touching the bright area of the sky.

Note, however, that the dark spots in the scene may look less exposed (this can look very good if the pattern is to be silhouetted).

When you touch a dark area, the camera illuminates the dark parts of the scene. That way you can see the color and detail in the dark areas of the picture. However, bright areas like the sky can look very bright (see below).

Touching to focus on different parts of the scene has a huge effect on the lighting.

However, you may not want the sharpness and brightness points to be the same. For example, if you want to go to the sky, you may want to focus on the pattern in the foreground.

iPhone offers an easy way to adjust the exposure after adjusting the focus.

Swipe up or down to adjust the brightness after pressing for focus. Swipe up to take a photo or down to darken it.

When the exposure levels look good, press the shutter button for such photos.

HDR stands for High Dynamic Range. Without HDR, your camera tries to capture all the details in a high-contrast scene.

In the photo below, you can see that the bright areas of the sky are completely white with no detail.

HDR allows you to create a well-lit photo with lots of color and detail in shadows and light.

Works by recording multiple scenes with different illuminance levels. These images are automatically combined to create an evenly exposed photo.

HDR is ideal for landscape photos with a lighter sky and a darker background. Allows you to capture stunning images, rich in color and detail.

USING HDR IN THE CAMERA APPLICATION

You actually have two options:

You can enable Smart HDR so that the camera can automatically take HDR photos when needed.

However, you can manually control the HDR setting in the camera application.

If you have any of the iPhone 11 models I would recommend using Smart HDR.

Well-lit images stunning are created on iPhone 11 by Smart HDR. The camera uses HDR only when necessary.

If you have an older iPhone, you can use HDR manually.

Because the HDR capability of older iPhone models doesn't always produce the best results. Sometimes a photo looks better outside of HDR.

Regardless of which iPhone you have, check the HDR settings under Settings> Camera.

If you want the camera to use HDR automatically, make sure Smart HDR (Auto HDR on some older iPhones) is enabled.

As soon as Smart HDR is turned off, the HDR icon will be displayed in the camera app.

Tap the HDR icon to toggle it on or off. (HDR is turned off when a line is drawn over the icon.)

If you want to control HDR manually, turn it on when you're shooting high contrast scenes. Otherwise, you may get overexposed labels as shown above.

Access to control multiple iPhone cameras: If you have an iPhone XS device or older, you will see a series of icons at the top of the screen.

These icons allow you to adjust the following settings from left to right: Flash, HDR, Live Photos, Timers and Filters.

However, some camera controls are hidden on iPhone 11 models. Tap the up arrow at the top of the screen to view the icons. Or pull the viewfinder up.

An icon type appears at the bottom of the screen.

These icons are, from left to right: flash, night mode (only visible in low light conditions), live photos, aspect ratio, timer, filter, and HDR.

(Note that the HDR icon will not appear if Smart HDR is enabled in Settings.)

Let's take a look at the settings that we haven't covered in this guide.

If you don't want to use the flash to illuminate the scene, turn off the flash setting.

You can take a photo in one of three proportions: square, 4: 3 (standard rectangle), or 16: 9 (width).

The square and 16: 9 aspect ratio cut out part of your image. For this reason, I recommend that you take photos in a 4: 3 ratio.

The countdown icon allows you to set the delay between pressing the shutter button and taking a photo. If you don't want to use the iPhone timer, make sure this setting is turned off.

You can use the filter icon to quickly change the color tone of a photo.

Many filters give your image an antique look. You can even change the photo to black and white.

You can also use or remove these filters when editing pictures in the Photos app. So it's usually best to take pictures without a filter and then experiment with them while editing.

Select the left welding filter for unfiltered storage.

Press the down arrow at the top of the screen to hide the camera control icons again. Or slide the viewfinder down.

CHAPTER TWO

HOW TO MOVE CAMERA APP TO DOCK

1) This area is known as the socket. Yes, you can add or remove applications from the Dock, but you cannot have more than 5 applications in the database.

2) Touch and hold the application icon until all of the applications on the screen are open. Then, tap and hold the app you want to move and drag it to where you want it to be installed. You can move a program off the docking station and add another program. You can also add an application folder to the docking station. Move one animation to another to create a program folder. When you have finished moving applications, press the Home button to stop the applications.

3) Note that you only have 5 locations in the dock. So if you want to use more than 5 applications in the Dock, create folders and place cards in the Dock.

APPLYING FILTERS IN PHOTOS FOR IPHONE 12

Filters in the Photos app are useful when you want to save a picture or photo that isn't what you expected, or when you want to change your mood and strive for a unique result.

- From the Home screen, tap the Photos app to open the app.
- Touch the photo that you want to filter.
- In the upper right of the screen, locate and tap the Edit button.
- Apply a filter to photos on iPhone and iPad by doing the following: launch Photos, tap the photo you want to edit, then tap Edit.
- Press the filter button in the middle of the submenu.
- Scroll and press the filter you want to apply.
- Touch Done.

Apply a filter to photos on iPhone and iPad, which will show you the following steps: Click Filter, select the filter you want to apply, and then tap Done.

When you're ready to take iPhone to a new level in photo editing, consider a third-party app that offers more options than the original photo app. The most interesting applications in the App Store include Prisma, Popsicolor and Olli from Tinrocket. However, you can stick to more traditional photo editing applications as they always have their own filters and effects to enhance your photos. Experimentation is the key!

APPLYING FILTERS WITH THE CAMERA APPLICATION

Apply live photo filters on iPhone and iPad step by step: press the filter button, select a filter, and take a photo as usual

Did you know that in addition to using filters in the editing process, you can also capture images with a filter already in use? These are known as "live" photo filters that can be easily accessed through the camera app. Live Photo Filters are a great way to see what an image will look like with a filter before you take a photo! It's great and useful when you want to create pictures as they are without having to edit them later.

HOW TO TAKE PHOTOS IN LOW LIGHT OR NIGHT MODE

You can use night mode to take pictures when the camera detects low light.

The following devices have Night mode available: iPhone 12 mini, iPhone 12, iPhone 12 Pro Max, iPhone 12 Pro, iPhone 11, iPhone 11 Pro and iPhone 11 Pro Max.

Night mode will be activated automatically when the camera detects low light. When the mode is active, the night mode icon at the top of the screen turns yellow. Depending on how dark the scene is, your iPhone can take a quick photo or a few seconds in night mode. The exposure setting can be changed.

For best results, keep the iPhone steady until the recording finishes. Place iPhone on a firm, stable surface or use a tripod for stability and control brightness.

If your iPhone detects movement while you are taking a photo, you can align the crosshairs in the frame to reduce movement and improve the shot. To stop recording in night mode in the middle of the recording and not wait for the recording to finish, just press the stop button below the slider.

HOW TO ADJUST THE RECORDING TIME

When recording in night mode, a number is displayed next to the night mode icon indicating how long the download will take.

If you want to try larger photos at night, choose the Night Mode option. Then use the slider above the shutter button to select Max, which will increase the recording time. When you take a photo, the slider counts down to the end of the recording time.

- ♥ Get a selfie in night mode
- ♥ Open the camera application.
- ♥ Press the front camera button.
- ♥ In front of you, hold up your iPhone.
- ♥ Take your selfie.

Night portraits are supported on iPhone 12, iPhone 12 Mini, iPhone 12 Pro, and iPhone 12 Pro Max.

CAPTURE TIME-LAPSE VIDEOS IN NIGHT MODE

In low light conditions, you can use the bedside table with the stand to record movies at longer intervals. Open the Camera app and drag it to the left until you see the time-lapse. To record videos, locate and tap on the shutter button.

Night Time Lapse is available for iPhone 12, iPhone 12 Mini, iPhone 12 Pro, and iPhone 12 Pro Max.

CHAPTER THREE

HOW TO USE PORTRAIT NIGHT ONLY

- ♥ Open the camera application and drag it in portrait orientation.
- ♥ . Follow the instructions on the screen.
- ♥ Press the shutter button.
- ♥ Night mode is available for iPhone 12 Pro and iPhone 12 Pro Max.

HOW TO TURN ON PHOTOS AND LIVE FLASH

When your iPhone is in Night Mode, Photos and Live Flash are not turned on. You can activate these functions manually. Note that enabling Photos or Live Flash will disable Night Mode.

When the flash is set to Auto, it will turn on automatically in low light conditions. To manually open the flash, press the up arrow in the viewfinder. Press the Flash button that appears under the viewfinder, then select On.

TO CHANGE VIDEO RESOLUTION ON IPHONE 12 CAMERA

- ♥ Start the camera application.
- ♥ Swipe left or right under the viewfinder to select Video or Slow Motion.
- ♥ You will notice that the dotted resolution and speed signs appear in the upper right corner. Tap any day to toggle between the image quality settings.

That's how it works.

IPHONE VIDEO RESOLUTION

Unfortunately, the new resolution and frame rate switches are static labels on devices other than the iPhone 11.

Pressing the resolution tag toggles between Settings → Camera and maximum video resolution on the phone. For example, if the default recording mode is set to 720p in the camera settings, tapping the label toggles between 720p and 4K. If the video quality is set to 1080p under Settings → Camera, the label rotates between 1080p and 4K.

However, pressing the frame rate indicator will display all frame rates (FPS) supported by the currently selected camera and shooting mode. Pressing a label on the camera surface rotates between 24, 30, and 60 frames per second if the image quality is set to 4K under Image Settings ‑ › Camera. When recording at 1080p, the frame rate display rotates between 30 and 60 frames per second.

In 720p recording mode, the frame rate is limited to 30 frames per second.

This extremely useful feature is supported on the iPhone 11 or later with iOS 13.2+ on the front and rear cameras in both normal and slow motion. These tags are also found on the camera surface of older iPhones, but only reflect the currently selected video resolution and the thumbnail mode, which are defined under Settings → Camera.

HOW TO CHANGE THE ASPECT RATIO

Apple has redesigned the home camera app on the iPhone 11 and the original iPhone 11 Pro to accommodate the various additional recording options on the new flagship phones. A particularly welcome change is the introduction of various aspect ratio capture methods.

How to change the aspect ratio of the iPhone 12

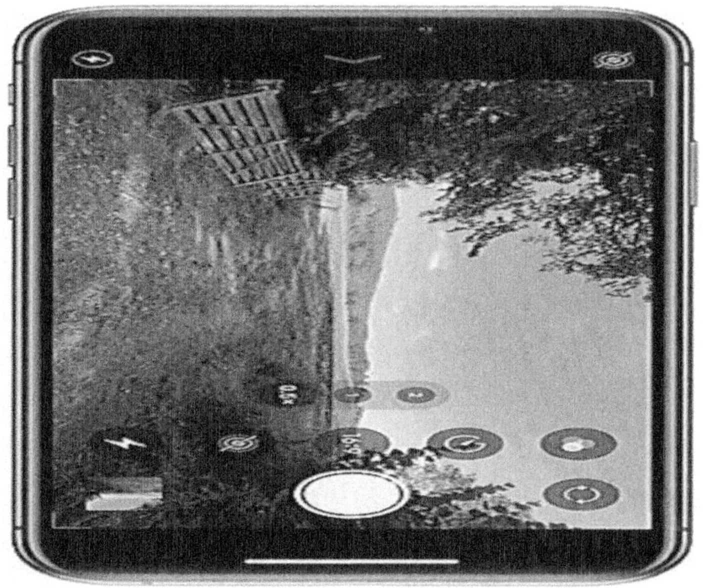

1) As with previous iPhones, the camera app only offers a 1: 1 capture function for Instagram-style photos called Square. This means that users can only choose different aspect ratios in photo editing mode.
2) On PhoneiPhone 11, PhoneiPhone 11 Pro and iPhone 11 Pro Max, users can choose between three aspect ratio options when

recording in the Camera app: 1: 1, 4: 3 and 16: 9 various download functions These steps are carried out step by step. Step.

3) Launch the camera app and tap the chevron icon at the top of the viewfinder (or on the side if you're recording in landscape mode) to reveal the hidden disc

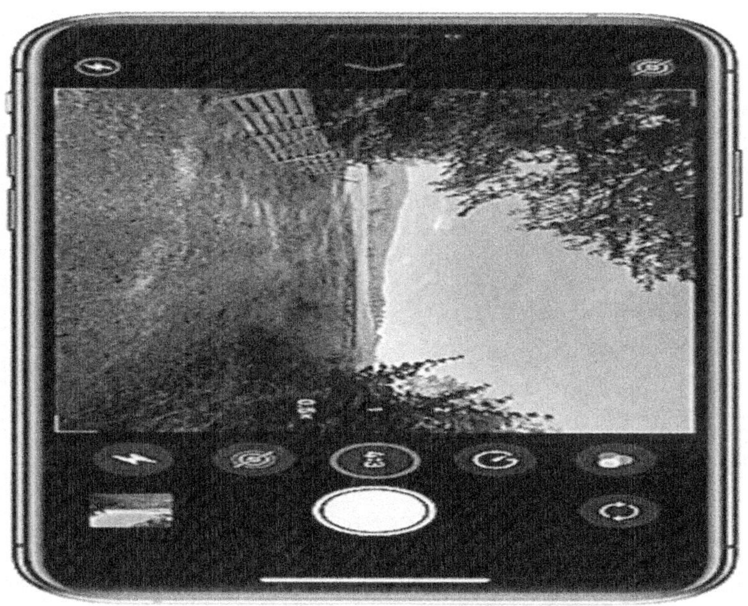

4) Press the 4: 3 button in the toolbox that appears just below (or next to) the viewfinder.

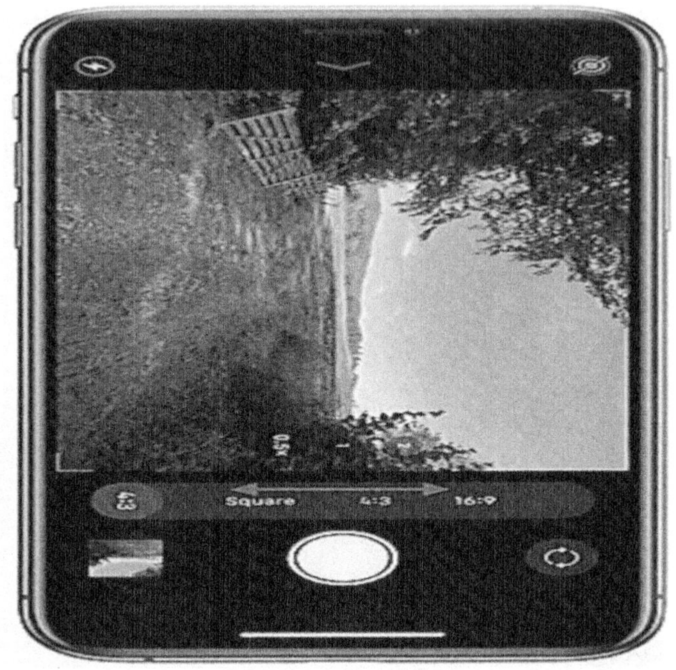

5) Select the desired aspect ratio from the drop-down menu for the 4: 3 button.

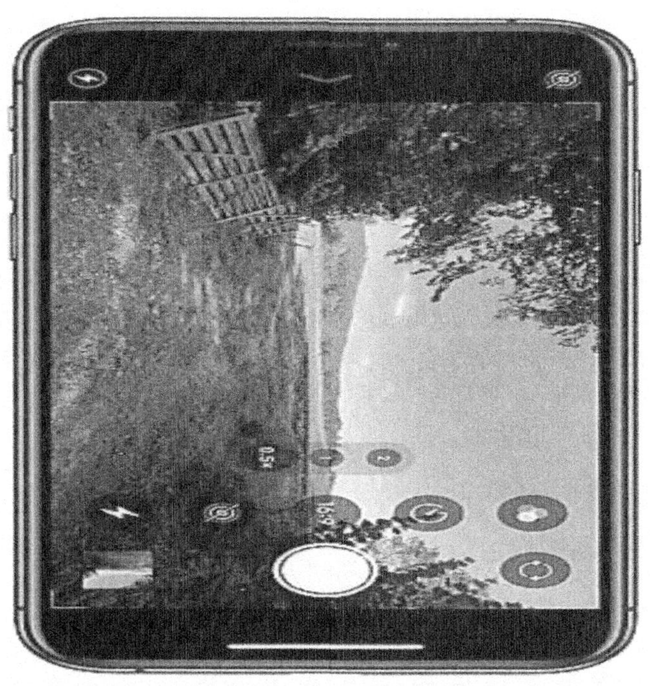

6) Continue recording.

Note that the 1: 1 and 16: 9 ratios do not go away. In other words, if you later decide that you want to go back to the standard 4: 3 field, you can cut that out again in the edit window.

DOLBY VISION HDR VIDEO RECORDING

All four new iPhone 12 series support a completely new standard for video recording: Dolby Vision HDR video.

You can enable Dolby Vision HDR on iPhone 12 for the best possible quality. This article will teach you how to enable and disable HDR videos on iPhone 12. We show some examples of HDR video compared to the normal non-HDR video. Then watch the file size to find out how much space HDR is taking up.

To turn the Dolby Vision HDR video on and off:

- Go to Settings and scroll down until you find the camera
- Click Download Video
- You can enable or disable HDR video at the bottom of the screen

Unfortunately, there's no easy way to toggle HDR video on and off right from the camera interface. So you need to go to the camera settings to use this option. With Apple, users can now quickly switch between 4K / 1080p and various frame rates right from the camera app. However, changing the HDR settings shows that the company believes that this is a much more powerful user function than it should be. a normal user. Monitoring by the camera application.

Apple has long argued that "no other smartphone can do this" in Dolby Vision HDR, saying, "in fact, even the cameras in the movie industry can't do that." Sounds like a big deal, doesn't it? Apple also explains that it will jump from 8-bit to 10-bit video so you have 60 times more color. Yes, that's 60 layers or 700 million colors!

How and where to watch Dolby Vision HDR videos captured on iPhone 12:

Right now the answer is a little complicated. Of course, you can watch HDR videos right on your iPhone. Then we tried sending the same file to OnePlus 8T and this phone couldn't play it. Instead, it showed a black screen.

There was no problem transferring the file while the file was playing, it looks blank and overly exposed, and YouTube doesn't seem to support this type of HDR content adequately.

This also applies to some TVs, where the content will play on some 4K HDR TVs but not others.

HOW TO SHOOT SLOW-MO VIDEO

A feature only offered by high-end cameras that are expensive is now available for iPhone 5s and later models - *Slow motion video*. It's easy to use, affordable, and fun. Here are the steps to download slowly.

Click the camera app to open it

At the bottom of the screen PHOTO, SQUARE, PANEL, etc. You can find texts such as.

Swipe right and you will see the SLO-MO

Start recording a slow-motion video by tapping the red record button

Press the shutter button again to turn off iPhone slow motion recording

When you stop recording, the recorded slow motion will be saved in the photo application. You can now specify which part of the clip should have normal speed and which part of the video should keep the slow motion settings.

HOW TO FIND RECORDED VIDEO ON IPHONE 12

To find all the slow motion videos in the slow motion menu, open the Photos app and go to Albums. Click the video you want to edit to view it.

To edit, click Edit to bring up the editing interface. The timeline is displayed below the video.

How to Slow Down Video on iPhone

In the middle, you will find 2 black thick lines. These 2 thick lines decide which part of the clip playback is slow. Drag the bars left or right to make the slow motion effect smaller or wider

Press the blue button at the bottom of the screen to check the editing

How do I edit slow motion videos on iPhone?

Some Important Facts About Slow Motion Video Recording on iPhone

Screenshot - You can take a photo while slowly moving from the iPhone. In the lower left corner of the screen, locate and tap on the white button. The high-resolution image is automatically saved in the Roll Camera folder next to the recorded video.

Record 1080p slow motion videos at 120 frames per second and save about 375MB per minute. The 720p slow motion iPhone at 240 frames per second consumes around 300MB per minute.

It is possible to slow down a video from normal video - slow motion video recording requires a slower video speed than normal. Slow video playback is usually possible, not the other way around. If you're trying to watch slow motion video from a normal picture, you get a bumpy video here and there with bounce frames. It's not a permanent video, it's like a series of downloads.

NORMAL SPEED VIDEO CONVERSION TO SLOW MOTION

If you recorded videos at normal speed on your iPhone and you want to convert them in slow motion or you can't record slow motion with your iPhone, you can use other programs to slow down the conversion. Here we can suggest some video speed change applications to convert videos to slow videos at normal speed.

1. SLOPRO

SloPro is a free tool for creating iPhone slow motion recordings. Start recording immediately after starting SLOPRO. When you're done, select a video from the library and hit the red edit button in the top right corner. Then use the crop and paste buttons to highlight the part of the video that you want to slow down. To set the slow motion option, it is recommended to choose between 500 frames per second and 1000 frames per second. You can slow down the video by 25%, 40%, or 50%.

When everything is set up, press Render and choose Optical Flow for the best settings. Finally, save. Save the full version in the video app and share it with your friends on YouTube and Facebook if you like.

The free version of SLOPRO has a watermark, which is a real downside. Download the full version of the application to avoid such problems.

2. *EXTREME SLOW MOTION CAMCORDER*

With watermark cuts, the free version of the iPhone Slow Motion Camera Extreme offers ten seconds of free recording time. There is no such limitation for the paid version. Although there aren't many editing options, you can choose a video from the camera or record a high-quality video by clicking the 50% mark. The video speed is reduced by 25%, 50%, or 75%. Click the music icon to add slow motion songs to the iPhone. When you're done editing, hit the share button and upload the slow video straight to the platforms to share with your friends. Social networks

HOW TO TAKE A QUICK TAKE VIDEO ON IPHONE 12

With iOS 14, you can use QuickTake to record video while recording without changing modes.

You can use the QuickTake camera on the following devices: iPhone XS, iPhone XR, and later models.

Press and hold the shutter icon to download a video

When you open the camera app, you will see the default capture mode. Select the shutter icon to take a photo. Press the arrow to set options like flash, live photos, night mode, countdown, and more.

To record a QuickTake video, simply press and hold the shutter button. Release the button to stop recording.

In iOS 14, you can hold down any of the volume keys to record QuickTake videos. If you've turned on Volume Up Burst, you can use the mute button to record a QuickTake video.

Swipe right to lock the recording

To continue recording video without pressing the button, pull the shutter button to the right, and release it. When the video recording is locked, the shutter button is displayed on the right. While recording a video, tap to take a photo. Tap the record button when you're ready to stop recording.

Swipe left to repeat

Drag and hold the shutter button to the left to take consecutive photos. Then release it to stop it.

In iOS 14, you can take a photo one at a time by pressing the volume down key. Go to Settings> Camera and enable Use volume for serial recording.

CHAPTER FOUR

HOW TO SEE BEYOND YOUR CAMERA FRAME

Look out of the box

For iPhone models with an ultra-wide (0.5x) lens, the camera surface shows what is happening outside of the picture you are taking. For a better photo, this can help you decide whether to resize your iPhone or switch to a different camera lens.

Custom Look Automatically application to your photos

When it detects a scene, the camera intelligently detects what you're photographing and adjusts the view to show the best of the scene. To disable this feature, go to Settings> Camera and turn off scene detection.

Scene detection is available for iPhone 12, iPhone 12 mini, iPhone 12 Pro and iPhone 12 Pro Max.

HOW TO ADJUST SHARPNESS AND BRIGHTNESS

Before taking a photo, the camera automatically adjusts focus and exposure, and Face Detection compensates for the exposure of multiple faces. IOS 14 allows you to refine and lock the report for upcoming downloads by controlling exposure compensation.

Just press the arrow and then touch and set the exposure level. The backlight remains locked until the next time the camera app is opened.

HOW TO TAKE A MIRROR STICKER

IOS 14 allows you to have a selfie mirror that will take pictures as you view them in the camera. To turn on the front camera with a mirror, go to Settings> Camera and open the setting.

HOW TO CAPTURE PHOTOS QUICKLY

IOS 14 lets you change the way you edit pictures with the benefit of faster capture so you can take more photos with the push of a button. To turn it off, go to Settings> Camera and turn off Faster Capture Advantage.

Take portraits to the next level

In portrait orientation, the camera creates a depth of field effects that allow you to create studio-quality photos that keep the subject in focus while blurring the background.

HOW DO YOU IMPROVE YOUR SELFIES AND EXTREMELY WIDE PHOTOS?

The lens setting automatically improves photos and becomes more natural when you take selfies with the front camera or with an ultra-wide-angle (0.5x) lens. To turn it off, go to Settings> Camera and turn off Lens Fix.

ADJUST A SLOW VIDEO SPEED

The easiest way to turn slow video speeds into normal ones on your iPhone is to use the pre-installed Photos app. All of the videos you recorded with your iPhone are saved here. Editing tools built into photos can speed up slow-motion videos. Just follow these steps:

1) Open the Photos app.
2) Tap Albums.
3) Scroll to Media Types and press Slow Motion.

4) Tap the video that you want to speed up.

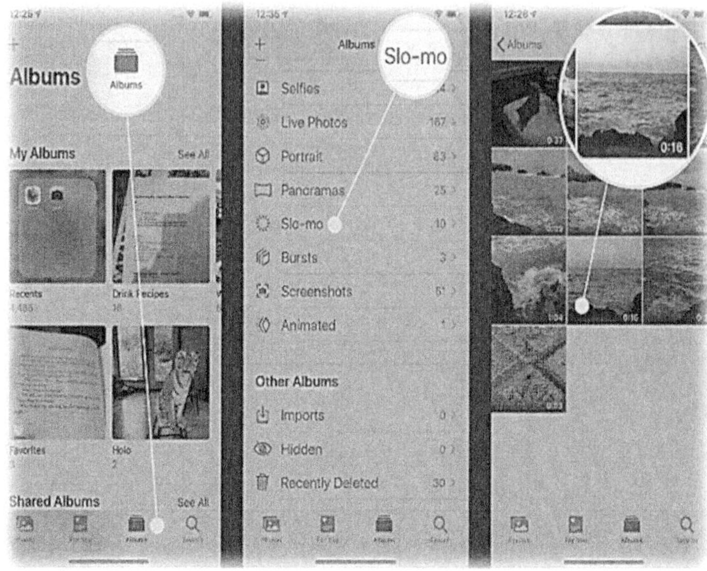

5) With the video open, press Edit.
6) At the bottom is a series of vertical lines. Show the video speed in this download location. Lines that are too close indicate normal speed, while lines further away indicate that this section is in slow motion.
7) Touch line by line and slide your finger over the slow motion area. All lines are replaced with a version that means normal speed.

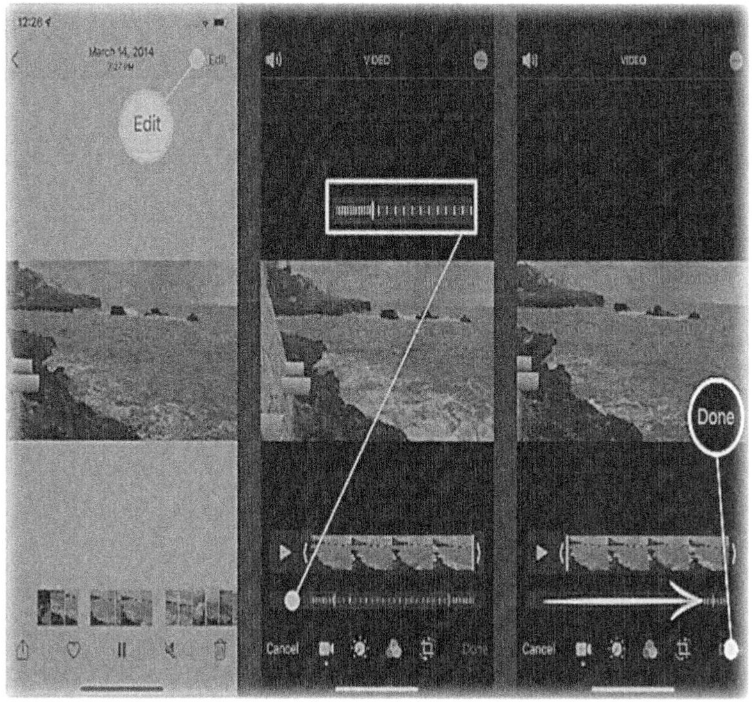

8) After changing the video speed, press Done to save the video.

9) Have you changed your mind and want to add slow motion to the video? Select the part of the video that you want to slow down so that it has the yellow line. Then slide your finger along the line until the section you want separates.

HOW TO SPEED UP VIDEO ON IMOVIE ON IPHONE

If you want movie editing apps to be a little more powerful than Photos, you can choose Apple iMovie (download iMovie from the App Store). IMovie has all kinds of video editing features including adding filters, titles, music, and more. You can also convert slow motion videos to normal speed. To speed up videos in iMovie, please do the following:

1. Open iMovie.
2. Click Create Project.
3. Touch "Movie".
4. Touch Multimedia.

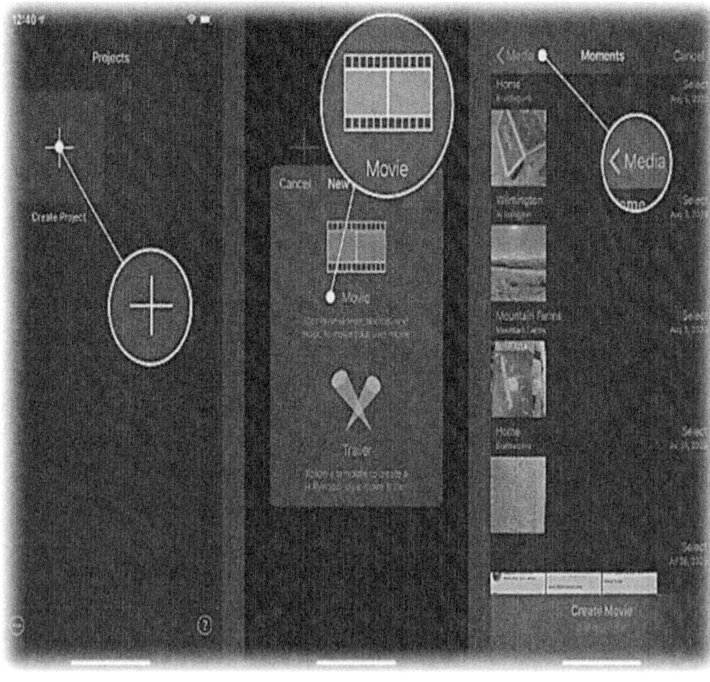

5. Touch Video.

6. Press Slow Motion.

7. Tap the video that you want to speed up. Then tap the check box on the pop-up menu.

8. Touch Make Movie.

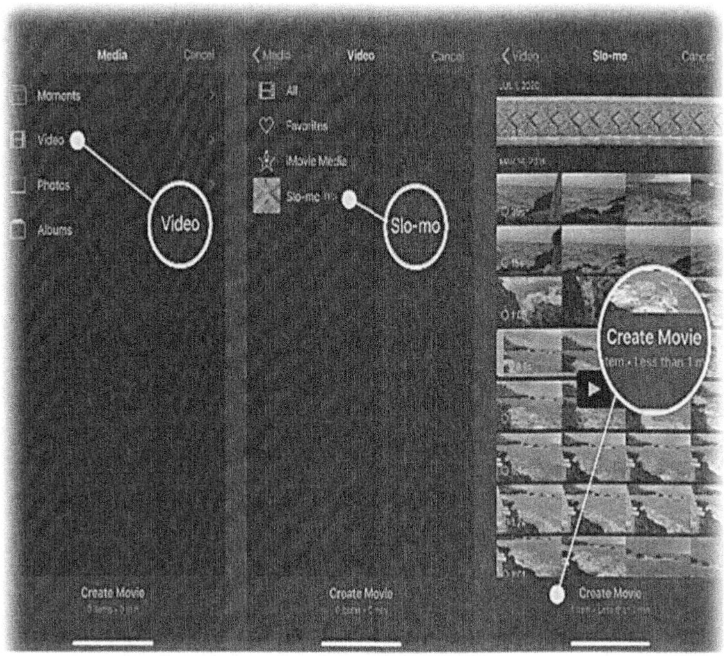

9. Tap the video timer to explore the editing options at the bottom of the screen.

10. Press the clock icon to open the playback speed control. Speed controls are a series of lines with a turtle representing slow motion on one end and a rabbit representing speed

on the other end. The number next to the rabbit icon indicates the speed of the video.

11. Move the speed dial so the number next to the rabbit is 1x. This is the normal speed.

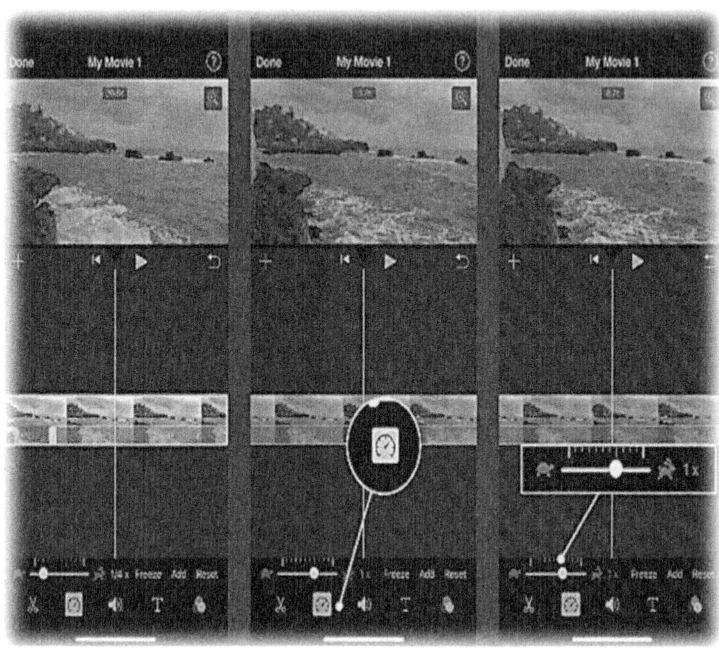

ADJUSTING THE VIDEO PLAYBACK SPEED

♥ Press Done to save the variable speed video.

♥ Press the Action button (arrow box on arrow) on the video screen to share, export, or anything else.

- ♥ Almost on the share buttons How Many Videos iPhone Can

- ♥ Want to learn more about video and video editing on your iPhone? We have articles on Record, How to Record Videos and Photos at One Time, and a lot more.

CHAPTER FIVE

HOW TO TAKE AND PROCESS LIVE PHOTOS

Capture photos that come to life when you touch them. Afterwards, select another important photo; add a fun effect, edit your live photo and share it with your family and friends then.

For Live Photos, your iPhone will record what happens 1.5 seconds before and after you take a photo. What you get is more than just a good photo. It is a moment recorded through movement and sound. You will get live photos just like traditional photos.

HOW TO TAKE A LIFE PHOTO

Open the camera app.

Make sure the camera is in Capture mode and Live Photos is enabled. When this option is enabled, a Live Photos button will appear on top of the camera.

Press the shutter button.

Live photos are included by default. You can turn off Live Photos temporarily or permanently.

HOW TO FIND AND PLAY YOUR PHOTOS

- ♥ Open the Photos app.
- ♥ Tap the Album tab.
- ♥ Scroll to Media Type and tap Live Photos.
- ♥ To open it, locate and touch one of the photos.
- ♥ Touch and hold the live photo playback screen.
- ♥ You can also enjoy live photos every time you unlock your device. As your lock screen wallpaper, just set it.

HOW TO CHANGE A KEY PHOTO

- ♥ Open the live photo.
- ♥ Click on Edit.

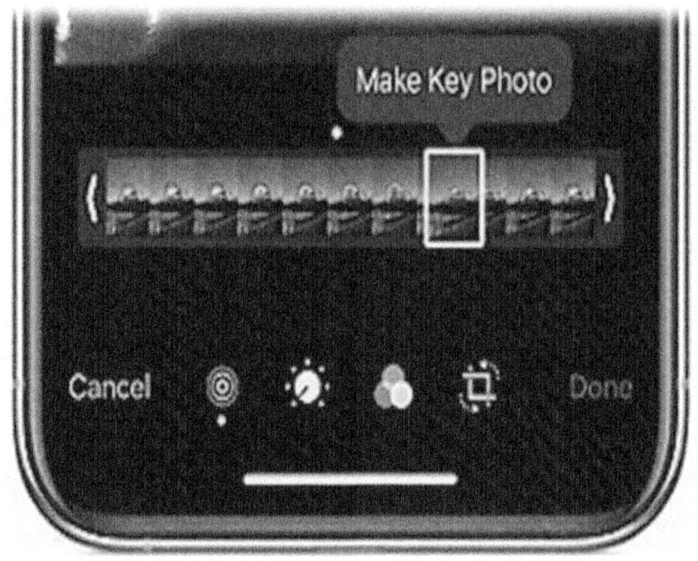

- Click the Live Photos button.
- To change the frame, move the slider.
- Lift your finger and tap Take Key Photo.
- Touch Done.
- You can also turn the live photo effect on and off. While editing a live photo, press the LIVE button at the top of the screen to turn the live photo off or on.

HOW TO ADD LIVE PHOTOS

Open the live photo.

Swipe up until you see the effects.

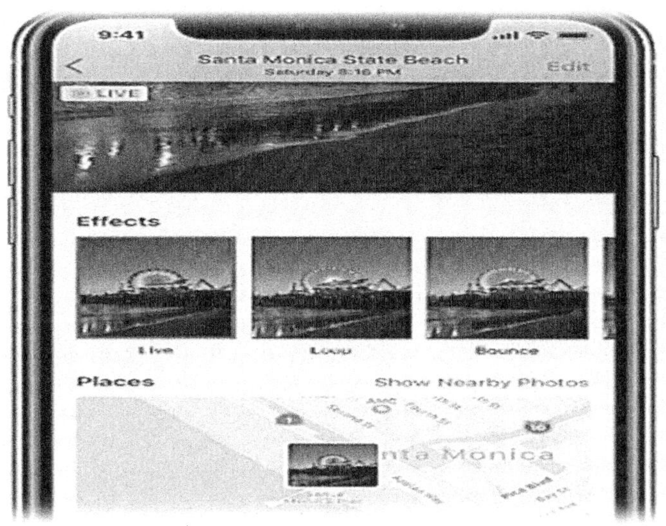

Choose from loop, bounce, or long exposure.

Loop: Converts a preferred live stream into a video loop. Pick an image yourself or check the For You tab to view photos that create wonderful loops.

Bounce: shake your live photo back and forth. Instantly play it upside down and view your live photo as it is.

Long exposure: recording time and traffic data. Create a beautiful effect that sometimes is only possible with a DSLR camera. Fireworks turn into glowing streaks in the night sky.

HOW TO EDIT LIVE PHOTOS

- ♥ Locate and tap on the Photos tab after opening the Photos app.
- ♥ Touch the live photo that you want to edit.
- ♥ Touch Edit and set it.
- ♥ When you are finished, click Done.
- ♥ If you edit the live photo in a third-party application, you may lose all of the live photo effects you have used.

HOW TO SHARE YOUR PHOTOS LIVE

- ♥ Open the photo you want to share, and then click the Share button.
- ♥ To share a photo instead of a live photo, tap Live in the top left.
- ♥ The method of sharing your photo should be determined. When you share an email with others, the live photo will be sent as a photo.
- ♥ When you receive a live photo via messaging on your iPhone, iPad, or iPod touch, tap to open it, and then press and hold to view it live.

If you're using Messages on your Mac, double-click Live Photo to open it. The live photo is played once. Click the LIVE button in the lower left corner of the photo to play it.

HOW DO YOU CLOSE LIVE PHOTOS?

Click the Live Photos button to turn off Live Photos. The bar above the Live Photos button means the feature is disabled.

The camera app will automatically open live photos. To permanently disable Live Photos, please do the following:

➢ Open the Settings application.
➢ Tap Camera> Keep Settings.
➢ Make sure the switch next to Live Photos is turned on.

HOW TO MAKE A SLIDESHOW IN PHOTOS ON IPHONE

Open the Photos app and select the album that you want to use in your presentation.

1) Tap the picture you want the presentation to begin on.
2) After selecting the first image, click the Split button in the lower left corner.
3) Scroll down and select Slideshow.

4) It will start automatically.

5) To adjust the slideshow settings, tap the screen, then tap the pause icon at the bottom of the screen.

6) Touch an option.

7) Here you can edit the theme, the music, the repetition speed, or the presentation.

8) When you have made your changes, click Done. He'll start playing.

9) To play an AirPlay slideshow on another device, press Pause again and select the AirPlay icon in the top right corner of the screen.

10) Tap the name of the device on which you want to play the AirPlay slideshow.

11) When you have finished playing the slide show, click Finish in the upper left to end the slide show.

12) Your settings will be saved the next time you want to play this album as a slide show. You can add filters to any photo in this album for an extra feel. Then polish the slide and prepare it for release.

DELETE AND HIDE PHOTOS AND VIDEOS

In Photos, you can delete photos and videos from your iPhone or hide them in a hidden album. You can also recover recently deleted photos. When you use iCloud Photos, any changes are saved across all of your devices.

Delete or hide photo or video

In Photos, tap a photo or video, and then do one of the following:

Delete: Click the Delete button to delete a photo from the same iCloud Photos account on iPhone and other devices.

Deleted media files are stored in the Recently Deleted album for about 30 days, where they can be restored or permanently removed from all devices.

Hide: Click the Split button, then click Hide in the list of options.

Hidden photos are moved to the hidden album. You can't see them anywhere else.

To turn off a hidden album so it doesn't show up in albums, go to Settings> Photos and turn off the hidden album.

How to Recover Deleted Photos or Delete Them Permanently

To recover or permanently delete deleted photos, do the following:

- Go to the Albums tab and tap Recently Deleted in the Tools section.
- Touch Select, then touch the photos and videos you want to restore or delete.
- Select Reset or Delete at the bottom of the screen.

HOW TO MANAGE ALBUM PHOTOS

- Tap the Photos application on the menu.
- Tap the Album tab.
- In the upper left corner, locate and tap on the + button.
- Touch New Album.
- Name the album and press Save.
- Touch the photos you want to add to the album.
- Click on Done.

HOW TO CREATE A NEW SHARED ALBUM IN PHOTOS

You can also use the Photos app to create an album that you can share with others. This is very useful when you want to create an album where you and other family members can view your photos and even add your own photos. See how to create it.

1) From your iPhone menu, tap the Photos app.

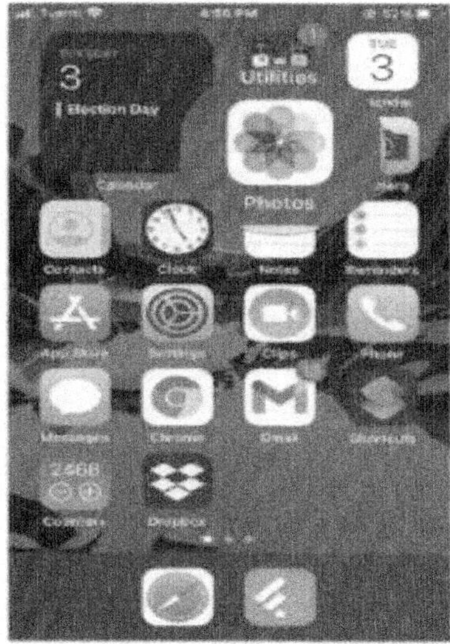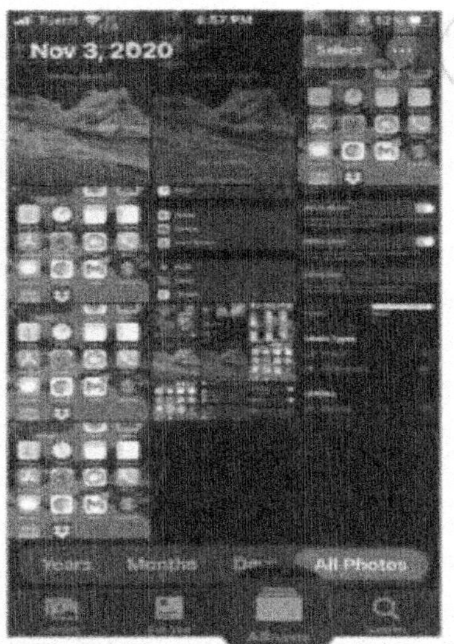

2) Tap Albums.
3) In the upper left corner, locate and tap on the + button.

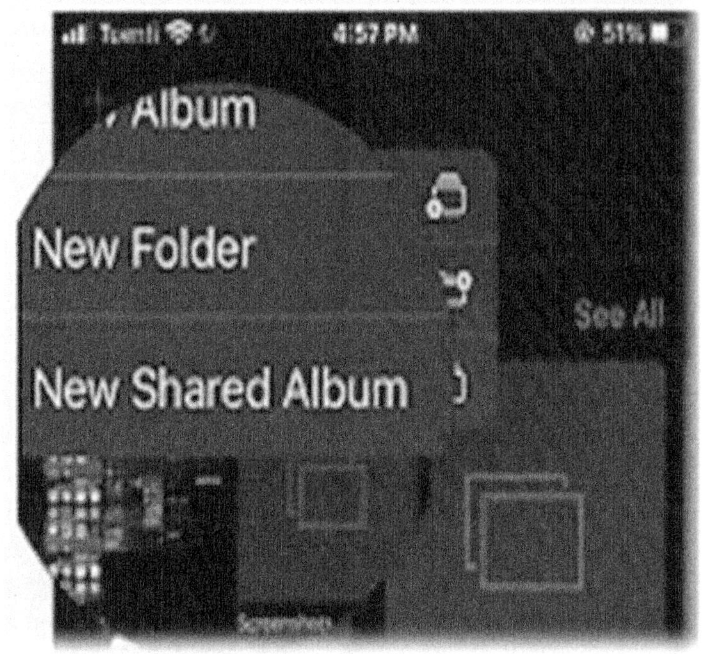

4) Touch New Shared Album.

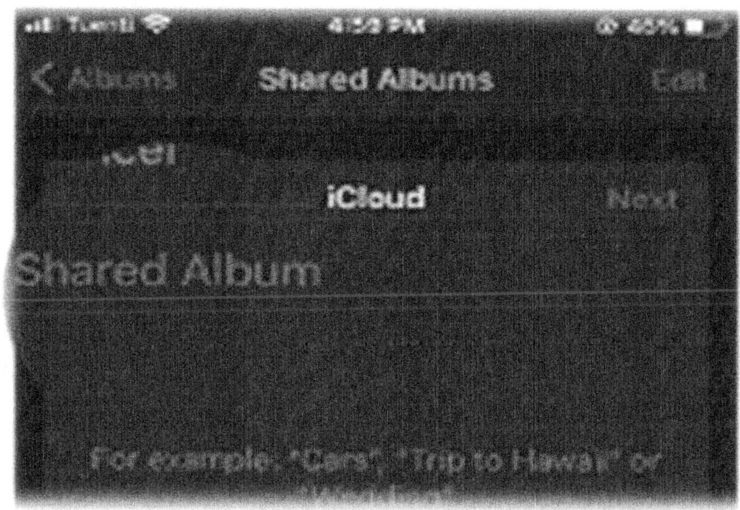

5) Enter a name for your album.

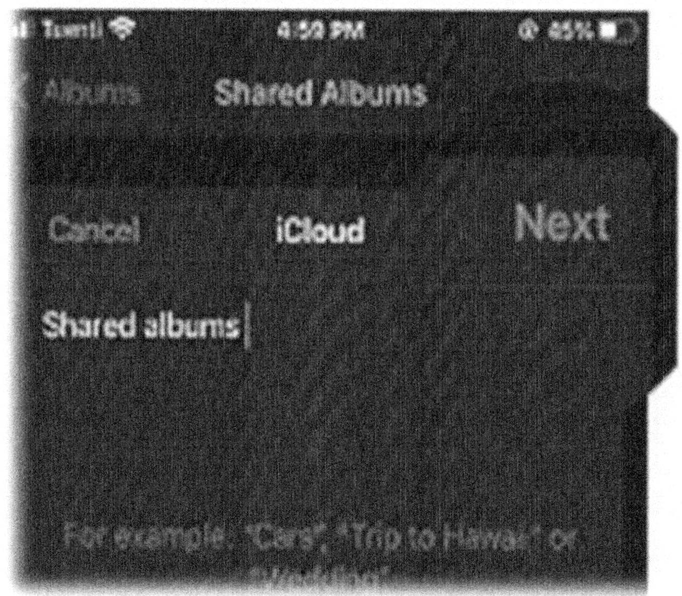

6) Touch Next.

7) The names you want to share the album with should be entered.

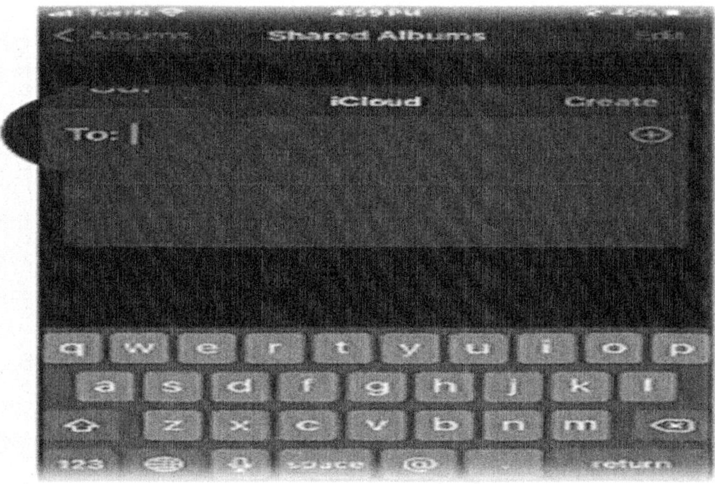

8) Click Create.

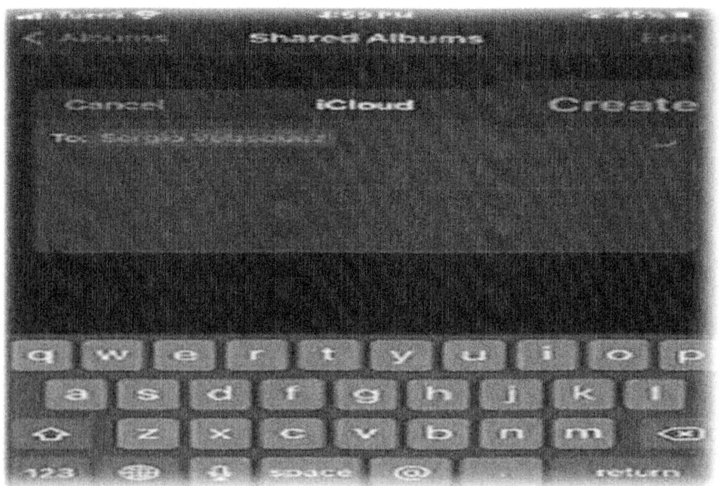

9) Tap a shared album.

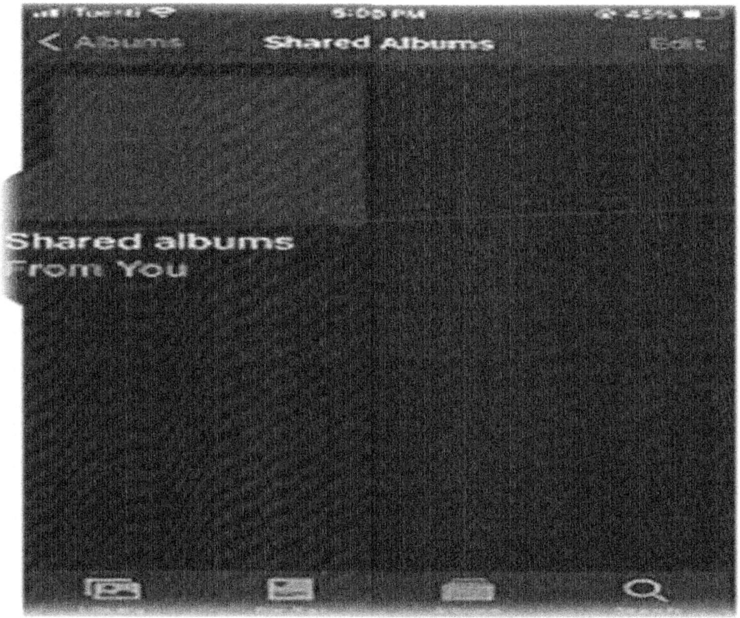

10)   Touch the + button.

11)Touch a photo that you want to add to the
   album.

12)   Touch Done.

13)   If you want, you can insert something
   that matches the pictures you added.

14)   Click Publish.

CHAPTER SIX

HOW TO ADD A PICTURE TO A SHARED ALBUM

If you really want to learn how to organize album photos on your iPhone or iPad, you need to know how to add photos to an existing album. Fortunately, it's very easy. Just follow these steps:

1) Open photos on iPhone and iPad.
2) Tap the Library tab.
3) Tap Days or All Photos.
4) Open Photos, tap Photos, tap Days or All Photos
5) Press Select.
6) Photos you are adding to the album should be tapped.
7) Press the Share button in the lower left corner.
8) Press Select, choose photos and then tap Share
9) Touch Add to Album or Add to Shared Album.

10)   Tap the album that you want to add photos to.

11)Click Add to Album and tap Album

12)   Your photos will then be added to the selected album.

HOW TO DELETE EXISTING ALBUMS IN PHOTOS

Creating and organizing folders is one thing; deleting unnecessary folders is another. This is very easy and only requires a few taps.

- Open the Photos app.
- Tap the Album tab.
- Next to My Albums, click Show All.
- Click on Edit.
- Select the album you want to delete and tap the icon to the left of the album.
- Click Delete Album.
- Touch Done.

HOW TO ORGANIZE YOUR PHOTOS

The Photos app makes it easy to organize and access your photos and videos. It can even give your photos a therapeutic look, and the built-in search intelligence will help you find what you're looking for quickly.

Photos are organized into libraries, albums, and searches. When you open iCloud Photos, your gallery will be updated on your devices. To find photos based on a place, person, object, or event, the advanced search capabilities make it easy.

Before you start

- ♥ Your iPhone's iOS version should be brought update, to the latest.
- ♥ Install iCloud on all of your devices.
- ♥ Sign in with the same Apple ID. Be sure to do that.

Library

Enjoy moments correctly displayed in the Library tab, then browse years, months, days, or photos. They will also bring live pictures and videos to life as you browse and surf.

Age: Search through the entire library of photos and videos you take every year. Then drag to scan.

Months: view many photos and videos from memories and places each month. Click the More for More button to share or play a movie made from your moments.

Days: view photos of the day to view some videos that will play automatically while playing. Tap and drag a photo up to see its location on the map and the contacts on it.

All Photos: Including screenshots and duplicate photos in the order they were taken, search your entire photo library.

With iOS 14, you can filter the screen to make it easier to navigate the library. You can select only photos or only videos to view. How to Filter what you see:

- ♥ Click the Library tab, then click the More button in the top right corner.
- ♥ Push Filter, and then select an option.
- ♥ Click on Done.
- ♥ To clean the filter, tap the Filter button at the top of the screen, then tap the Filter button, select an option, and then tap Done.

HOW TO TRANSFER VIDEOS AND PHOTOS

Below is a list of all the ways you can transfer photos:

Transfer photos and videos from iPhone to iPhone with Airdrop

AirDrop is a standard service developed by Apple for iOS and macOS for the quick and easy transfer of files such as photos, videos and more between iPhone, iPad, and Mac. Works on WiFi and Bluetooth networks and only works with iDevices with iOS 7 or higher or Mac OS with OS X Yosemite. In other words, you can use AirDrop on an iPhone 5 or later, a fourth generation iPad, or a newer fifth or fifth generation iPod touch. Now let's see how to copy photos from the old iPhone 5/6/7/8/10/11 to the new iPhone 12.

Step 1. Start the Control Center on both iPhones. Swipe/draw your fingers up from the bottom of the screen for not earlier than iPhone 8 users. From the top right corner of the screen, you can also swipe/draw your fingers down.

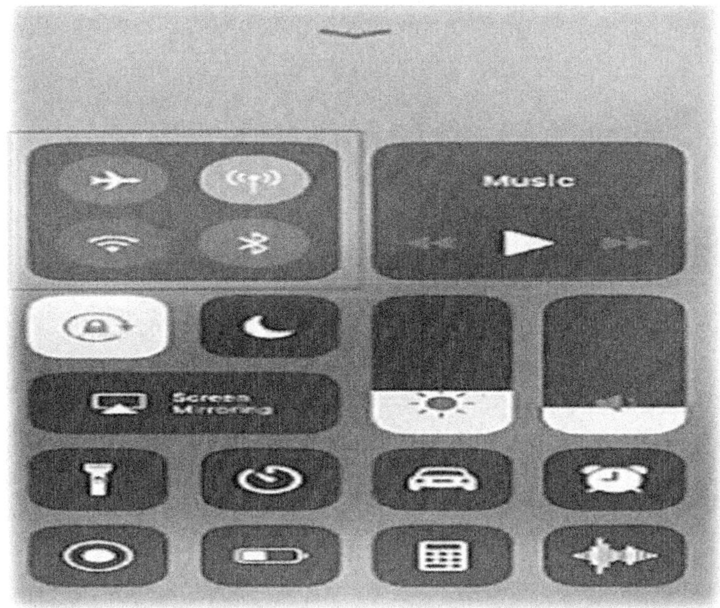

Step 2. Press and hold the wireless control panel in the upper left of the control center.

Step 3. You will see the AirDrop option and press. Then choose who can send you via AirDrop by clicking Dismount, Contacts Only, or Everyone. I recommend it to anyone.

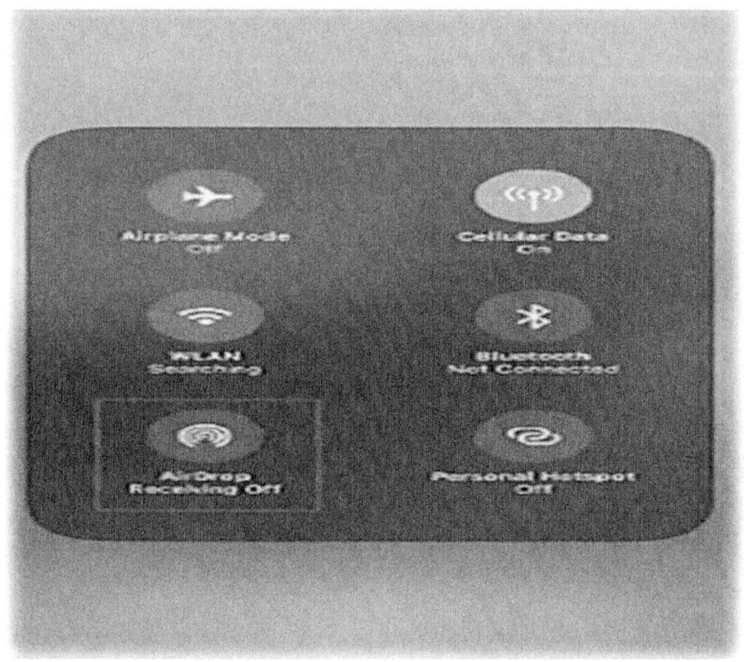

Step 4. Now go to the Photos app on the iPhone and choose the photos that you want to move to a new iPhone.

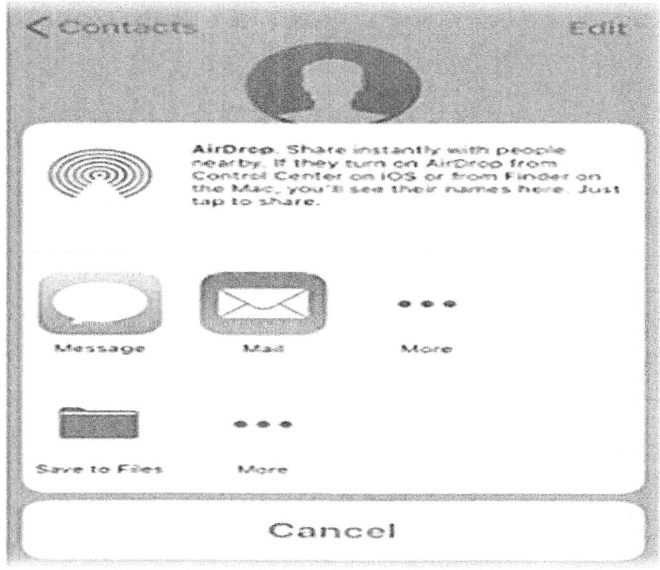

Step 5. Once selected, tap the "Share" button on the lower left corner of the iPhone screen.

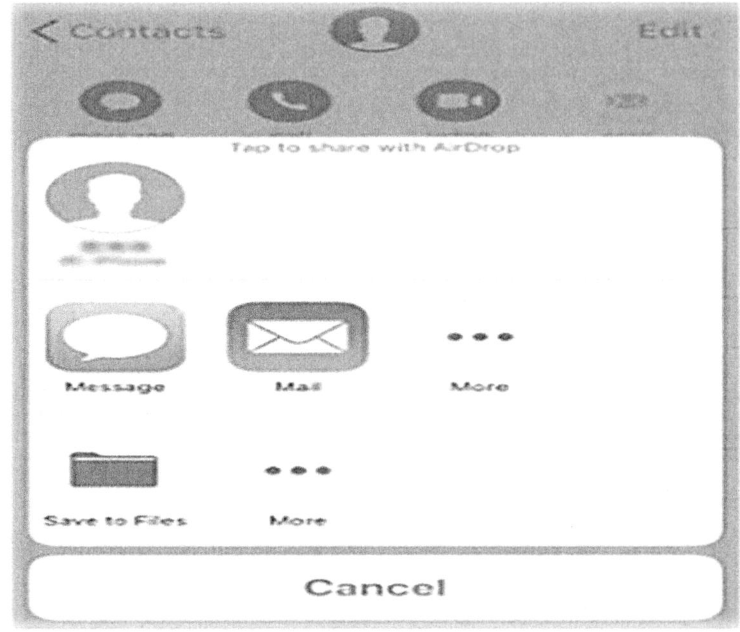

Step 6. Tap your new iPhone 12 and when the recipient appears on the AirDrop bar, selected photos will start transferring to your new iPhone 12.

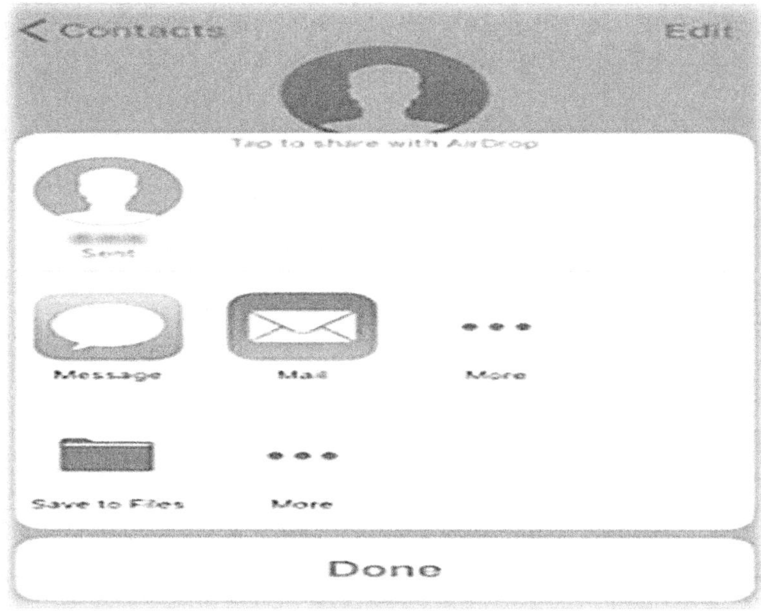

Note: If you have a lot of photos to send, this method may not be a good choice.

Videos And Photos Transfer Between iPhones using iCloud

ICloud can be one of the easiest ways to transfer files like photos between iPhones. This method requires a strong and stable internet connection. When you copy photos using iCloud, you need to make sure that both iDevices are connected to the same Apple ID. Here's how to transfer photos from one iPhone to another iPhone using iCloud:

Step 1. On your old iPhone, tap Settings> Enter your name> Select iCloud> Tap Photos.

Step 2. Select Optimize iPhone Storage or Transfer and keep the originals. Your iPhone then uploads photos to iCloud.

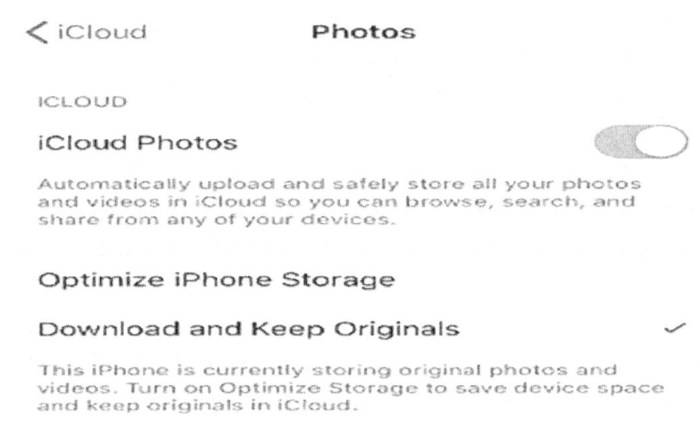

Step 3. When done, open the new iPhone 12 and enable iCloud Photos.

Step 4. Open the Photos app on a new iPhone, select All Photos and you will see all the iCloud photos that have been transferred from your old iPhone.

Using MediaTrans to Transfer Photos between iPhones

MediaTrans is a professional iPhone photo transfer software. This method can be the fastest and easiest way to transfer photos from one iPhone to another. Allows you to easily click all or selected old iPhone photos on a new iPhone. Most importantly, MediaTrans allows you to export HEIC photos in JPEG format. I also like to use MediaTrans to copy photos from iPhone to Windows 10. Simple Steps to Transfer Photos to New iPhone Using MediaTrans:

Step 1. Download and run MediaTrans on your computer and connect your old iPhone to your computer with a USB cable.

Step 2. Click the Upload Photo button, then select all or specific photos on your old iPhone and click the Export button to backup the selected photos to your computer.

Step 3. Disconnect the old iPhone and reconnect the new iPhone 12 to the computer.

Step 4. Click Transfer Photos on the main interface again, then click the Add Photos icon to import the selected folders to your computer. Tap the Sync button to transfer old photos from iPhone to new iPhone.

Using iTunes to Transfer photos Between iPhones

iTunes is the last resort to copy photos between iPhones as it is a little tricky to do. In addition, this method has a number of limitations:

This method isn't available if you've turned on iCloud Photos.

You can only transfer photos to iPhone (iCloud photos, photos synced from your computer, not shared photos)

Photo sync in iTunes will replace your existing iPhone photo library. In other words, you could lose some of your backed up photos.

Here are the steps to transfer photos from iPhone to iPhone 12 using iTunes:

Step 1. Get your old iPhone connected to your computer and open iTunes. Click Summary in the left pane after you have selected your iPhone in iTunes.

Step 2. In the right pane, under the Backup section, click this computer, then click Back up Now.

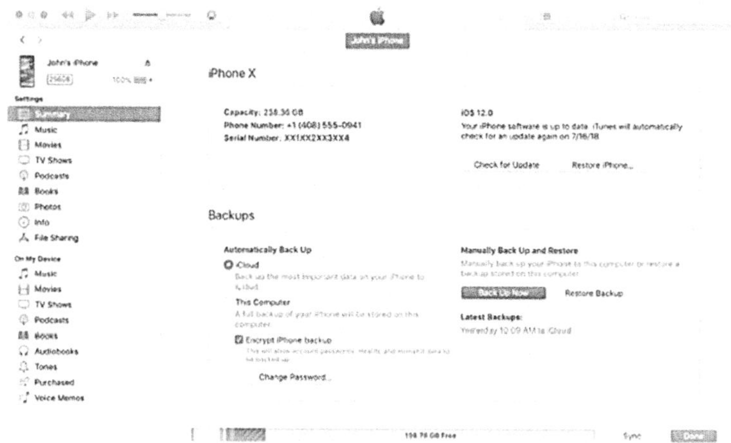

Step 3. When you turn on your new iPhone and iOS Assistant Setup, you will be given the option of "Restore" from iTunes Backup. Just select them.

Step 4. Connect your new iPhone to the same computer and open iTunes again. Click Summary in the left pane after you have selected your new iPhone in iTunes.

Step 5. Click Restore iPhone in the right pane and then select I Agree. When the process is done, all of your photos will be on the new iPhone 12.

CORRECTION OF COLOR CAST IN PICTURES

Would you like to customize the color of your iOS picture? It's as easy as making the cake as there is a processing tool that you can use to get it done in about two seconds. First, find the photo that you want to change and then click the "Edit" button.

Edit button to adjust the color of the photo

Once the tools appear, click the Apple Customize button highlighted below.

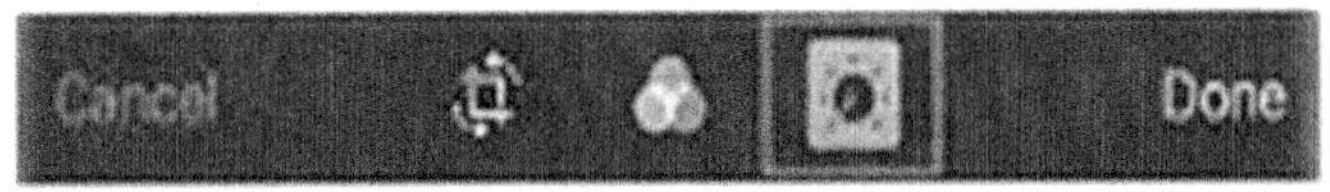

The adjustment tools for light, color and black and white will open.

Clicking the arrow next to any of these sections will reveal more complex options. We're going to press the arrow next to "Color" to get to "Post".

Then select "Post" to make changes and you will see a little line that you can move back and forth. Moving to the right makes the image cooler (see below) and warmer to the left.

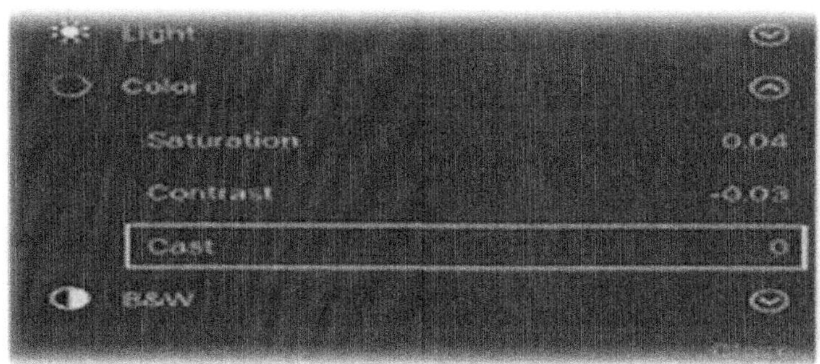

Drag the Post slider to adjust the color in iOS photos

HOW TO REMOVE OBJECT FROM IMAGE

Touch Retouch has several tools for removing objects from photos.

113

The quickest and easiest option, however, is the Quick Brush tool. Just rub the object and it will go away!

Such as the sky or water, this tool is best for removing objects surrounded by empty spaces or small objects.

To edit something in an image with the Quick Brush tool:

1) Open the TouchRetouch app and tap Album. Find the photo you want to edit and tap the photo to open it.
2) Tap Quick Fix at the bottom of the screen. Next, make sure the Quick Brush tool is selected.
3) If you want, you can press Settings and use the size slider to adjust the size of the brush. The brush is a white circle inside the green circle.
4) It's also a good idea to enlarge the item you want to remove - especially if the item is small. This will ensure the correct selection of elements.
5) To zoom in, place two fingers on the screen and spread them apart. You can move to a different part of the picture by moving with two fingers.

6) Now run your finger over the object that you want to remove.

7) You cannot see the object under your finger because your finger is covering the area you selected. When you touch the screen, you will see a white circle with the area selected.

8) The selected area is displayed in green. If you drop your finger, the object will disappear!

9) You will notice that the object has been replaced with the surrounding pixels. In this case, the pixels from the surrounding water replace the race.

10) In most cases, the application is excellent. However, if you are not satisfied with the result, tap Cancel (back arrow) at the top of the screen. Then try again to brush the object.

11) You can keep brushing other areas to remove as many elements as you want. In the following example, all colored buoys in the water have been removed.

12) When you are happy with the result, it is time to save your picture.

13) To save, tap the export icon (square up arrow) in the top right corner. Then click Save as a Copy.

14) Your edited picture is saved in the Photo app on the iPhone.

15) Tap Back in the upper left to close the output screen. Then tap the homepage icon to choose another image to edit.

Remove the unwanted lines from the image

You can easily fix these issues with a ridge removal tool.

This tool uses innovative technology to identify and remove thick, thin, straight, or curved lines.

♥ To remove streaks from a photo, open it in TouchRetouch.

♥ Tap Remove Lines at the bottom of the screen, then select the Remove Line tool.

♥ Remove only part of the line, not the whole. Choose Segment Extractor.

♥ Choose whether the line you want to remove is medium, thin, or thick after tapping Settings at the bottom right.

- To remove an entire line, simply slide your finger over part of the line. It is not necessary to mark the entire line. And you don't have to be precise because practice will find the line.
- (Note that if you select the Remove Trace tool, you must mark the entire line segment for removal.)
- As soon as you drop your finger, the animation will disappear from your photo!
- If the line has not been completely removed, press Cancel and select the line again.
- Be sure to save your changes after removing the line.

Get large or irregular shapes

In this case, the tools mentioned so far may not be suitable.

But don't hesitate to remove large or irregular objects!

The Object Removal Tool is an easy way to select complex shapes.

In the example below, I've removed the jumper from the photo. So only his reflection remained and he created an interesting and mysterious composition.

Open the image in TouchRetouch and click Remove Items. At the bottom of the screen, you can see three object selection tools: brush, lasso, and eraser.

Brush and Lasso tools are used to select objects. You can use the eraser to deselect the randomly selected area.

In most cases, the brush tool is your best bet for selecting elements.

Zoom in and overlay the item you want to remove. Press Settings to adjust the brush size.

The lasso tool works a little differently. Do not rub the object with this tool.

Instead, draw a straight line around the edge of the object. When you drop your finger, all of the hair will be selected.

When your object is large, the lasso tool becomes very useful. This means that you don't have to rub the entire object with your finger.

Check this carefully after choosing an item. Zoom in and check the edges.

If you make a mistake and choose too many wallpapers, don't worry! Go to the eraser and clean the areas you want to break off.

Once you've selected it correctly, click the scroll icon in the lower right corner. The selected element disappears!

When you're through, do not forget to save your changes.

Clone details from one area to another

The ultimate tool in TouchRetouch is the Clone Stamp Tool.

Cloning allows you to manually copy pixels from one area to another.

This is different from other tools that automatically replace the object with pixels in the area.

The Clone Tag can help you spot errors or repair a damaged background by removing an object.

It is also useful for removing objects with precision when other retouching tools do not give good results.

In the example below, I didn't get good results when I removed the flower underneath with an object extractor. This happened because the flowers were side by side.

So I cloned the part of the blue sky above the flower below with the clone seal.

You can also use a cloned stamp to copy objects into a photo.

In the following example, we copied the birds in the photo with the clone stamp. The extreme bird adds more drama to the picture.

Open the photo in TouchRetouch and hit Clone Stamp. Make sure you select the brush tool at the bottom of the screen.

Touch the object or area you want to reproduce (in this case one of the birds). The circle shows the "starting point". Press Reflect to reflect a cloned object horizontally, vertically, or diagonally.

Now color the area where you want the cloned content to appear. When brushing, the pixels at the point of origin are copied into the area to be deleted.

In the example above, the bird was cloned from the circle of the starting point in the second part of the photo. The double bird looks in the opposite direction because the view is set horizontally.

If you are not satisfied with the result, click Cancel or use the eraser to delete the cloned item.

If you want, continue with the above process to clone more objects in the image.

When you're happy with the editing, save the image.

Top tips for proper item removal

Knowing how to remove something from an image will greatly increase the editing capabilities.

However, you need to be careful to get realistic and accurate results.

Here are some of the best tips for great results.

Leave free space around your subject

In general, results are best when there is free space around the item you are trying to remove.

The sky, water, snow, fields and walls are the ideal bases for lifting objects.

When you remove an object, the pixels in the empty area around the object replace the object. However, if there is too much detail about the subject, it will be more difficult (but not impossible!) To get realistic results.

Small items are easier to remove than large ones

The smaller the particle, the easier it is to correct mistakes.

You can select small items quickly. And usually, there is more free space around them.

Large parts can be removed, but removal usually takes a little longer.

Magnification of the object

Make sure to zoom in by pressing out two fingers to properly lift objects.

Upon closer inspection, you can pick a clearer topic.

The more precisely you make your choice, the better the result.

Use an eraser for a more expensive choice

When choosing composites, check the selection edges.

Then use an eraser to erase any areas of the background that you shouldn't be selecting.

Deleting the wrong area will improve the end result.

If it fails, please try again!

You may not always get perfect results the first time you treat it. However, this does not mean that you cannot remove an object from the photo.

If the first step fails, click Cancel and try again.

Try brushing to cross a slightly different area of the object. Or try another editing tool.

You may need to spend a little more time editing images with complex objects or backgrounds.

CHAPTER SEVEN

IPHONE CAMERA TIPS AND TRICKS 12

Your iPhone has a powerful camera and a number of interesting features that can help you create beautiful photos. With your phone with you, you can instantly turn any situation into a photo shoot. But do you know how to take full advantage of iPhone camera settings?

USE THE LIVE MODE FOR SOUND AND MOVEMENT

Instead of freezing for a moment and taking photos, you can use Live Photo with iPhone camera settings to capture movement and sound. This camera function is ideal for capturing special moments that don't look like the normal picture.

Look for the circle icon at the top of the screen to use the live photo setting on your iPhone. If it crosses that line, it means it is off.

Note that when you use this camera feature, the device will automatically record 1.5 seconds of video before and after you press the shutter button. Press and hold for a few seconds while pulling on the camera.

To play a photo live, go to the Photos app, open it, and hold your finger on the screen to view it. You can even use some effects to make it more unique.

Open your live photo and swipe up to access the effects. You can choose between a loop, a jump, or a large exposure. The loop turns your live photo into an endless video loop. Bounce plays your live photo back and forth like in Boomerang. Extended exposure blocks any movement and is the perfect way to recreate the silky effects of waterfalls or rivers.

Adjust the focus to erase images

The iPhone camera has a great depth of field. This means that it's good to stay strong in the foreground and strong in the background. However, this does not mean that you no longer need to focus. You may get a blurry image that you otherwise cannot use.

Every time you take a photo with the device, wait before pressing the shutter button and set the focus point first. After shaping the frame, tap the screen that you want to adjust the focus on (this should be your subject). A yellow area indicates the focus point.

If you don't register in the studio, the environment will likely change. Your iPhone camera will be redirected automatically. Allows you to manually lock the iPhone camera, focus, and exposure to keep the settings. To do this, tap and hold the yellow square that marks the focus of your photo. After a few seconds, you will see the AE / AF lock icon at the top of the screen. Tap anywhere on the screen to unlock the feature.

Of course, sometimes you need some time to concentrate on the watch. But at least you can get a clear picture in the end. Make a habit of touching the screen before pressing the shutter button.

Manually adjust the report for more control

The iPhone camera will automatically adjust the exposure for you. However, this isn't always useful, and your photo is too dark (no exposure) or too light (too much exposure). What should you do when this happens?

Use a slider for lighting. This tool allows you to skip the iPhone's lighting settings and adjust it yourself.

You can use the exposure slider for a number of reasons. The most important thing is to adjust the brightness with it. However, you can overexpose/remove your shots for special effects like the silhouette shown in the photo above.

The exposure slider only appears when you touch the screen and select the focus area. Before making any adjustments, make sure you see the yellow box. If there's a yellow box on the iPhone screen, you'll see a sun icon next to it. Slide your finger up or down to change the lighting.

In real-time, you'll see the scene dark or light to find out how much to adjust. This is one of the iPhone's hidden camera settings, and most of them don't even know they're there.

Use Lattice Lines For Complete Assembly

Some photographers find it difficult to understand the meaning of the composition.

Fortunately, there are simple rules of composition you can apply, such as the rule of three.

The third rule divides the frame into a 3 x 3 grid and shows where the subject will be placed in the photo. This guide should be easy to follow, but what if you can't imagine the lines in your head?

The good news is that you can access one of the iPhone's camera settings, the grid feature, to take the photo. On the iPhone, go to Settings, select the Camera tab and enable the network. When you activate the function, lines will appear on the screen just in front of the scene you want to record.

All you have to do is determine the main problem with these beagles or determine where any of them intersect on the internet. Press the shutter button and your perfect composition is ready!

Update your picture with filters

Like many people, you are probably using Instagram / VSCO filters a lot more than the iPhone camera offers. However, using a native photo color application offers several advantages over third-party programs.

The first benefit is that you can use iPhone filters in live recording mode too. This means that you can use your preferred settings while recording.

First, open the Camera app and tap the three-tier icon in the top right corner of the screen. If you have a newer version of the iPhone, you'll need to tap the arrows at the top of the screen to access additional camera settings like filters, timers, or night camera mode.

Then just select one of the available filters and start recording!

Photos also allows you to change a predefined image at any time without affecting the image quality. To do this, go to the Photos app and tap the three-circle icon. Then select more filter options to change the filter.

Unlike third-party apps, your iPhone won't turn off the filter of the previously used filter. This way, you will not get an excessive photo with unnatural colors.

Record the action in sequential mode

When you have an animated subject, it can be difficult to pinpoint when to record it.

How do you make sure you don't miss the moment it happens? Well, you can hold your breath and hopefully hit the shutter at the right second ... or you can usc the burst feature.

You don't need to change any iPhone camera settings to allow continuous shooting. Holding down the shutter is all you have to do. On a newer iPhone camera (11, 11 Pro, or 11 Pro Max), you need to press the shutter button and immediately move left to take vertical photos or pull up in a horizontal direction.

The device will then take a picture until you touch the screen with your finger. The burst mode takes about 10 frames per second.

You can use the burst download feature for action shots where changes are made quickly. This is the best way to attract children, animals, or people to run, jump, walk, dance, or ride a bike. You can also try while taking the recognized photos. Here you can record the displayed moments.

When you're done, you can choose the best photos and ignore the rest. Open the Photos app, press Burst to open it, and choose the Select button at the bottom of the screen. Select the photos you want to save, click the Finish button in the top right corner and choose Keep Favorites Only.

Outdoor photo of a girl jumping on the sidewalk when she drops an iPhone

Use a timer

The timer is another important function in the camera application. You can use this camera function for a variety of purposes, such as B. for self-portraits or group portraits. You can also turn it on when taking landscape or night photos to prevent the camera shake.

You can find the iPhone timer in the top right corner of the screen or by pressing the up arrow. Pressing the icon will display the 3 and 10-second countdown options.

When taking self-portraits or group photos, choose 10 seconds. This gives you enough time to get into the frame before activating. If you're shooting landscapes and nights, the 3 second option works fine.

Always look for a solid surface to stabilize your iPhone while using the timer function. If you think you will be using the timer a lot, bring at least a mini tripod.

Use the auto-timer setting on the iPhone to take a picture of a female model

Use the crop tool to select an aspect ratio

In the age of social media, you can no longer limit yourself to 5: 4 or 4: 3 rectangular photos. Today you need the flexibility to experiment with 1: 1 square and other aspect ratios. The easiest way to do this is by using the iPhone clipping tool.

First, open the Photos app and select the picture you want to edit. Then tap the crop tool (square arrow icon). You can cut the file manually, but it is easier to choose the aspect ratio you want.

There are many options when choosing a ratio. The most common are 5: 4, 5: 3.4: 3, and 3: 2 for rectangular images.

You can choose between 7: 5 and 16: 9 for panoramic photos. If you want a square picture for Instagram, go for 1: 1.

Learn how to use the photo, square, plate, and other lenses

The disadvantage of editing is that it can affect the quality of the file. To keep the resolution of the iPhone camera, select the aspect ratio you want in the capture modes.

At the bottom of the camera application screen, you can choose between Photo, Frame and Control Panel, among other things. The default setting is the photo that creates a 5: 4 picture. Choose a square mode for Instagram with an aspect ratio of 1: 1. You can select the clipboard for an aspect ratio of 16: 9. The phone will resize the screen in live view to show the desired aspect ratio.

However, if you want to reduce the panoramic photo from 16: 9 to 7: 5, you will need to use the crop tool. The same applies to cropping pictures 5: 4 - 4: 3 or 3: 2.

Of course, the iPhone offers more photography options than the photo, frame, and clipboard. However, we combine them because if you don't want to crop the images, you will need them.

If your iPhone camera has more lenses, you have even more options to improve the quality of your photos. If your iPhone has two lenses and is older than iPhone 11, you have wide-angle and telephony functions. The iPhone 11 has a wide-angle and an ultra-wide-angle lens, while the 11 Pro and 11 Pro Max come with three different lenses for ultra-wide, wide-angle and telephoto settings.

When you open the iPhone camera app, you'll see numbers under the box. These are zoom options that you can use to switch between different lenses. Pressing the 0.5x option gives you an extremely wide-angle lens that can capture larger landscapes, buildings, or city lines.

Pressing the 1x button opens a wide-angle lens suitable for most photo settings. If you switch to 2x telephoto, you can view distant objects carefully. You can use this camera function in cases where it is not possible to physically approach the subject.

HDR recording for better exposure

Sometimes situations arise where neither automatic nor manual adjustments cannot turn them on properly. Such situations are often high-contrast lighting such as cloud cover, sunrise, and sunset.

Turn on HDR (High Dynamic Range) at the top of the screen in harsh lighting conditions. When you turn it on, the phone will ask you to take three pictures with different levels of lighting.

The first is normal, the next two are lighter and darker. The device then sews them together to create a vivid image with the right lighting.

If you have an iPhone 11, there are two additional camera settings on that device that you cannot control: Smart HDR and Deep Fusion. Both try to use lots of pictures taken in a short amount of time to get the best and to maximize the fine details like hair, fur, and texture in the photo.

To turn off Smart HDR, go to iPhone camera settings and toggle the switch off. There is no

Deep Fusion Camera Setup Key, but you can disable it by opening iPhone Settings, selecting the Camera tab, and enabling Out of Frame Capture.

USE THE PORTRAIT FUNCTION TO INFLUENCE THE DEPTH OF FIELD

An impressive feature of the iPhone 7 Plus and newer models is the portrait mode. Enables the capture of blurred backgrounds with two cameras and intelligent software.

To check portrait mode, open the Camera app, and tap Portrait at the bottom of the screen. The camera detects and automatically blurs the background.

If the app says you are too close to the camera, drag until you are at the appropriate distance.

Unfortunately, there is no vertical function in the iPhone 5 and iPhone 6 settings. However, if you want to try bokeh on your photos, you can choose third-party applications like the Tadaa SLR.

USE THE LIGHTING PORTRAIT FOR A STUDIO EFFECT

In portrait orientation, you can also use lighting to change the brightness of a photo. When you tap the iPhone camera screen, you can make the picture look like it was taken on stage or even in the studio.

To use portrait lighting, you must first select portrait mode in the camera application. You will find the following lighting effects at the bottom of the screen:

- ♥ Natural light
- ♥ Studio light
- ♥ Light contour
- ♥ Stage lights
- ♥ Scene light only

If you don't want to add lighting effects, choose the default natural light setting for iPhone. If you want to create whimsical portraits, you can try Contour Light. You can choose Stage or Studio Light for professional results.

Printed in Great Britain
by Amazon